Abandoned Parents, the Devil's Dilemma:

Causes and Consequences of Adult Children Abandoning Their Parents

By

Sharon A. Wildey

2014

Copyright © 2014 Rev. Sharon A. Wildey, Esq
All rights reserved.

How sharper than a serpent's tooth it is
To have a thankless child!

King Lear Act 1, scene 4, 281–289

Table of Contents

Table of Contents 4
Author's Foreword 7
INTRODUCTION 8
WHAT THIS BOOK IS AND IS NOT 10
Estrangement vs. Abandonment 11
   A distinction of terms 11
GENERAL OBSERVATIONS OF THE CAUSES OF PARENTAL
ABANDONMENT 12
THE MORAL AND ETHICAL DILEMMAS OF ABANDONMENT OF PARENTS
 18
TEMPTING EXPLANATIONS 22
CAUSES OF ABANDONMENT AND ALIENATION FROM PARENTS 24
   Cause No 1 - A Simple Breakdown 24
   Cause No. 2 Third Party Interveners 28
   Cause No. 3 The Dynamics of Emotional Disarray 39
   Cause No. 4 Traumatic Events 43
   Cause No. 5 The Dependency of Elderly Parents 45
   Cause No. 6 Failed Adult Children 47
   Cause No. 7 Unresolved Generational Trauma 50
   Cause No. 8 A Flawed Match 54
   The Injury 56
   Reasons why recovery is difficult 60
   Leaving Your Abusive Children: The Devil's Dilemma 72
IT SEEMS LIKE IT IS A PROCESS 78
HEALING BEGINS 81
   Hope and its role in your recovering life 82
   The normal process of ostracism and it's awful consequences 83
   First Educate yourself about the abandonment as a shared
   phenomena. 84
   Next use your imagination to take the pain down a notch and get
   yourself started 85
   Next you will need to change how your brain is thinking about your
   abandonment 87
   Deal with your emotions – all of them 90
   Very important to get your life under control 91
   Meditate, meditate, meditate and yoga 93
   Find a spiritual practice 94

IN THE DEPTHS OF PAIN GET OUT AND LOOK UP 95
   Avoid emotional charged activities 95
   Try to stop making the "crazy" model 96
   Posters, web sites, Face book, notes, cards, ... 97
   Avoid triggers and if can't avoid them embrace them 98
   Sudden meltdowns 100
   Friends, family, therapists and clergy 102
   Linguistics can change the world 103
   Build another family 104
   Write out a personal belief statement 104
   Avoid the terminal question 106
   The difference between a happy life and a meaningful life 107
   Expectations great and small 107
SPECULATION AND FINAL WORDS 109
APPENDIX 112
   A MESSAGE TO ADULT CHILDREN Who Have Abandoned their Parents 112
   Who is informing you? 112
   Do you seek true freedom in life? 113
   The consequences of your actions 113
   What happens to your own children 114
   Where are your parents or have you lost track of them 114
   Why should I? 115
List of Abusive Behaviors Perpetuated by Adult or Younger Children On their Parents 117
Bibliography 120
Web Resources 124
Facebook Resources and Page Titles 125
END NOTES 126
Author's Bio 130

Author's Foreword

Some years ago, I needed desperately to understand what happened to my family and to the children that I loved and cared for all of my life. Like most parents, I thought I had done the best I could do with what I had to do it with. There was little help available to me other than some initial writings on Parental Alienation set in the context of divorces. Without much success, I continued my search and over a period of years, I began to take notice of similar stories that had begun to surface here and there. I started a Facebook page on the subject, I heard from other parents and began to find commonalities and finally a picture emerged out of all the chaos that others have been experiencing.

I am a lawyer by training and I have used my skills to accumulate facts, formulate some hypothesis and draw some conclusions. This is a first effort – tentative steps toward understanding. There is hope here. Perhaps not the kind of hope we wish for, but the kind of hope that allows us to live with meaningfulness, the kind of hope that helps get us out of bed every day and try again. Most importantly, I discovered that I was not alone.

INTRODUCTION

This book is dedicated to the growing phenomena known as abandonment of parents by adult children. Abandonment is a form of abuse. Abandonment is ostracism. Abandonment of parents by adult children is violence. Abandonment of parents is not limited to the elderly. This social ill has gone by many different names such as targeted parents, alienated parent syndrome and elder abuse. By whatever name it is called, it is at its root shunning: the act of terminating critical social and personal relationships. Shunning is the intentional act of harming another by silent bullying. It is more common that we would like to believe.

Abandonment, walking away, neglect, or minimizing is natural to the human being as a primitive and intuitive way of solving problems. In the context of family, it's fundamental purpose and orientation is to relieve the adult child of what he or she finds unacceptable or inconvenient in their lives. Abandonment is abusive, torturous and if sustained over a period of time produces within the parent severe psychological and physical pain of such severity that the parent often develops serious mental and physical disorders and brain damage. It can and often does produce early death. Mental health resources have been late in diagnosing these phenomena and largely without adequate means to resolve the consequences to either the parent or the child or future generations. There is little information to report the effect on the adult children who do the abandoning but logically there must be serious consequences for them as well.

This book proposes to offer an approach to defining the phenomena, attempts to outline some causes and some initial resources for the parent(s) that are aggrieved by the conduct of their children. If there is comfort in numbers, parents should know that this seems to be a global problem that is cross cultural unrelated to wealth, education or country of origin. Finally, there are included here some resources and some ways to identify the growing estrangement in parent/adult child relationships before a complete break occurs. In the end the purpose of the book is to begin discussion of a growing issue that contains, within its silent boundaries, horrendous grief and pain. The mission of the book is to place one tiny pebble on the beach of hope, understanding and peace.

WHAT THIS BOOK IS AND IS NOT

This book is not a scientific study written by a social scientist. I am a lawyer and a pastor by training and therefore have some sense of critical thinking and observation. In coming to some of the conclusions, hypothesis and lists, I have poured through thousands of stories of abandonment, read books, opinions, blogs, support groups and web sites. My intent is to start a dialogue about this socially destructive force in motion all over the world. Please understand when you read this book, it is not social fact you are reading, it is an opinion based on observations and stories told to me. With that said, I hope what I have written helps form a basis for discussion and awareness.

This book is not written for adult children who abandoned or are estranged from their parents. I have included an appendix, which contains a message to you. However, you will not find much help here for your issues – whatever they may be. You will not find a balm here to support your rationalizations or your justifications for your conduct.

Estrangement vs. Abandonment

A distinction of terms

Before we go on to talk about causes, I would like to make a label/word distinction here between estrangement and abandonment for the purposes of this book. The emerging literature uses both terms interchangeably but there, I believe, is a difference distinguished by the behavior of the adult child. Estrangement might describe a simple drying up of the parent child relationship. There is no animosity or torture or direct hatefulness. There simply are fewer and fewer conversations, fewer letters, missed holidays all related to less and less points of reference in their respective lives. This is often caused by geographic distance or the end of life aging of the parents coupled with the business of work and family of the adult children.

Abandonment, on the other hand, is characterized by hurtful comments, physical or mental hatefulness. (see appendix which list a variety of abusive behaviors) where the intent of the behavior of the adult child toward the parent is to be cruel, to scapegoat or to banish. It usually is fueled by a core belief that the parents are guilty of a variety of short fallings and that a future relationship of any kind would be harmful to the adult child or his/her family. This core belief is held in absolute firmness almost approaching religious fervor in its impenetrability.

GENERAL OBSERVATIONS OF THE CAUSES OF PARENTAL ABANDONMENT

First, and let's be clear about this – parental abandonment is abuse and it follows the model of other kinds of physical and psychological abuse. Most importantly, it is a moral and ethical failing on the part of the adult child. There may be psychological diagnosis that can be made about the adult child who lives this hate filled life, and perhaps should be made, but first and above all it is a moral failure and in some cases even evil. Quite simply it is the wrong thing to do, a wrong action to take and places the adult child into a precarious environment that speaks to who they are, what they value and the nature of their character. There is not a crueler action to take against another human being than ostracism, abandonment and alienation and especially when that other human being is your parent. What makes an adult child or any age child take such cold, calculating and out of cultural norm action against the people who gave them life, support and nurture in their minorities - people who fed them, educated them, protected them and spent a good deal of the family resources to help them grow?

We know that this very behavior - abandonment and other forms of abuse - is common and perhaps the most common ending of the parent/child relationship. We know that it is cross cultural. From Japan to Iraq to Latin America, parents are being abandoned and abused and not due to any extreme social pressure such as war or famine. It is costing millions of dollars for governments to care for these parents not to mention the strain on the medical systems for the treatment of the emotional and physical disorders caused by this painful assault on their body and soul. We know that it is historical. In all of the world's major religions there is an admonition against abandonment and abuse of your parents. In fact it is more than an admonition, it a responsibility to respect and honor parents. It seems it is fair to say that without the presence of this common conduct there would have been no reason to build in an admonition against dishonoring parents.

Today's adult children who are taking these actions are quite possibly the ones who find some way to avoid measuring their conduct by "rightness" or "wrongness". Although it is hard to imagine how an adult child manages to justify not seeing her parents for 30 years, ignoring all attempts and pleas from the parents to just see them one more time before they die. It is not uncommon for the adult children who abandon their parents to lie, fabricate abuse stories, libel and slander their upbringing without so much as a blink. Shakespeare noted many years ago that taking someone's good name is to take their only treasure.

The next general observation is that the relationship is inconvenient and no longer meaningful to the adult child regardless of the causes. Quite simply there is nothing in it for the adult child anymore. Perhaps distance contributes to this problem as well. Simply stated when the adult child lives in California and the parents live in Illinois communication on a daily or weekly basis becomes difficult. The ability to transfer information about the daily lives of the other becomes too time-consuming, and as a natural consequence, communications are limited to perfunctory and obligatory or crisis oriented speech. The basis and the emotional connection begin to dwindle and eventually disconnects. We are all living under the delusion that once there is a parent/child bond it is somehow magically there forever because of some hormonally dictated urge. It can and will dwindle over time from lack of communication and from lack of dependency. Often the adult child's needs for relationships are very different and are satisfied more completely by their peers. Hence, peer relationships become more important and provide more helpful information about negotiating life. Peer relationships are often less "loaded" with the difficult history of growing up and therefore more easily negotiated. In evidence of this kind of relational abandonment take a look at how television characterizes parents: annoying, interfering, disruptive, unwelcome, clueless, ignorant at least uninformed, and most of all irrelevant. Only recently have television programs shown parents of adult children in a positive light in "Blue Bloods", Tom Selleck's program, where generational relationships provide guidance, sponsorship, protection and wisdom. No more Partridge Family or Father Knows Best.

Just as interesting the parents provide a much needed target for blame. In a time when life styles of young people are more complicated, lonely and alienated, when young people are under constant stress at work, financial difficulties and suffer from a lack of intimacy, when their lives are filled with a generalized angst that is often experienced as anxiety then blaming is historical man's best ointment. And who better to blame. This is most profoundly demonstrated in the common scenario when parents offer a suggestion on child rearing and that suggestion is met with a tirade of blame language about how the parent made worse mistakes. The tirade is often out of portion to the suggestion made. Scapegoating is a necessary and convenient tool for negotiating a hostile environment and it is often the parents who are targeted. Expendability is the hallmark of today's parent/adult child relationships.

This split becomes more obvious when the dependency shift begins as parent's age and a social and traditional burden is perceived by both as a shift of responsibility to the adult child. Those responsibilities and burdens are challenging at best, an interruption to the adult child's life and commitment to others and a burden without an emotional connection. It is often times yet one more burden placed on an adult child who is burdened beyond capacity in the first place. So avoidance is the best solution and coupled with a generalized complaint about how that parent "failed" them as a child is all that is needed to justify walking away. The proof is lying in nursing home beds all across the nation as day after day passes and not a visit, a letter or a telephone call from an adult child. If telephone calls are made they are most often made to the nurses for a brief run down on how Mom is doing. And this, just in case someone in their peer group asks how Mom is. This daily horror is kept as a conspiratorial secret by the nursing homes, the clergy, the nurses and aides and doctors. These professionals well know the physical and mental consequences of this kind of loneliness and emotional pain but they dare not speak for fear that the patient will just be moved to another facility. Depression is the most undiagnosed illness present in nursing homes today and all the better to keep the patients obedient and quiet.

Finally, all abandonment, in the face of desperate attempts by the parents to connect with their lost child, seems to have one underlying motivation and focus and that is a homicidal intent. The adult child has socially and psychologically "terminated" their parent. The child continues in life as if the parent is physically dead. They do not think of them, seek out information about them or remember them at holidays or birthdays. It is as if the slate has been wiped clean long before the actual physical death. This "death" is complete and impenetrable. Any effort to mediate or reconcile by anyone inside or outside of the family is met with complete denial and often anger at the intervener. These children do not seek therapy for any angst associated with the loss of their parents. They do not seem to grieve the loss of the parent. The only observable defect in their persona is that they often do not do well in adult life. They generally are not happy and have a sense of emptiness which is never connected to the loss of a relationship with their parents. What happens to the children of these adults is yet to be fully determined but what a powerful model for them.

We do know that the ultimate purpose and aim of abuse is to terminate the life of the one being abused whether that termination is spiritual, emotional or physical. The more intentional the abuse becomes, in the sense that the behavior is planned and designed to inflict pain, the more the behavior is motivated by the desire to terminate the life of the parent. There are no exceptions to this motivation. In fact, many parent abusers fanaticize about the death of the parent. Some become titillated at the idea of their parent's death often smiling and smirking when it is brought up in conversation. Often adult children will laugh about their parents attempt to reconcile with them. They often speak of a parent in past tense terms and boast about not knowing if the parent is still alive or not.

"I haven't been able to speak to my oldest daughter in 4 years. When she found out I have an incurable kidney disease on Mother's Day 4 years ago she texted me to "DIE! DIE! DIE! You deserve it!" Right out of the blue. It devastated me. I have no idea where she is coming from and she has cut all ties with me and my grandchildren, one of which I raised from birth to 5 years old. She is now 19. I haven't seen any of them in 10 years. It is heartbreaking and unfair and there is nothing I can do about it because she has blocked me from Facebook and I do not have her current address or phone #. Her sister will not get involved for fear she will stop all contact with her as well. I raised her to be a Christian and I have prayed and prayed about this but have found out that this is a 'silent epidemic' in America and I am not alone in this. That doesn't help much as I love my daughter very much and my grandchildren and am at a loss for words to explain it or console myself. Maybe after some time of growing up some more will change things for her. Hopefully so."

THE MORAL AND ETHICAL DILEMMAS OF ABANDONMENT OF PARENTS

A growing economic and human concern around the world and across cultures is the abandonment of parents by their adult children. Mostly this is public in the elderly as it is more visible when the parents are infirm. But the hidden parental abandonments are just as prolific. Adult children are just walking away from their relationship with their parents and often with a vitriol of blame and harshness. The cost of this abandonment in economic terms is staggering but in terms of human pain and misery it is immeasurable.

The official issue of elder abuse and abandonment as defined by various governmental units is vague and limited primarily to physical abuse or neglect. Remarkably the US government is unwilling to say two things that are relevant to our inquiry: First, government is unwilling to say that abandonment of the elderly without physical violence or neglect is abuse; and secondly, government is unwilling to say that adult children have a legal obligation to support their parents both financially and emotionally.

Meanwhile emergency rooms, bus stations and two bit hotels are filling up with older parents who have been dropped off with the promise to come back later. And it is done without a second thought. Sometimes these adult children just keep letting more and more time lapse between phone calls or visits. Separation by physical distance adds to the problem and makes an easy excuse to not go and see them. Again all relationships weaken over time even our most precious ones.

Parents become more and more useless and the tasks that they used to perform for their children are no longer in demand. Advice is not needed, childcare, sustenance is not needed, and the companionship is just something else to add to the stress of the family life. The parent becomes a "nuisance", a word defined as: "an annoying or irritating person or thing".

Perhaps it is nature's way of stress reduction—a kind of narrowing of stimulus. The fact is that abandonment is a seemingly natural process of terminating relationships that no longer have anything valuable to offer. The cultural taboos against abandoning parents are disappearing all over the globe. Parents as they age are becoming expendable. It is as if they have become diseased and the healthier community needs to isolate itself from them just like biblical lepers that were thrown into colonies of miserable existences.

Ethically speaking there is nothing in it for the adult children to continue in relationship with their parents. There is everything to gain by not doing so in terms of the expenditure of time and energy and sometimes resources. Most importantly there is no downside for abandonment. There is no longer any community imperative to provide for your parents. The way adult children treated their parents used to be one of the biggest measures of an adult's worth and character. No longer. No one loses a job, fails to get a promotion, bears a bad mark against their name, or suffers any exposure to the greater community for this behavior. It's free from all disparity. In fact it is rare that anyone is ever asked about the welfare of their parents. It is merely assumed that the subject is taboo.

Honor your father and mother is the 5th commandment, the first one of the 10 that speaks to the issue of relationships among people. It is couched in terms of a blessing: "so that you will enjoy the land given to you by your Holy Father". In its reversal it is an admonition to a disobedient child.

So what is lost? Obviously what is lost is a lifetime of experience and wisdom, help with the household tasks and rearing of the children, a built in sounding board, and the first community of existence. Generational relationship is what keeps us from being alone in the world. On a public level the economic cost is staggering. When the family abandons a generational task i.e. taking care of their elderly, the government must pick it up in the form of welfare. Unless of course you live in India where the abandoned are simply left on the streets and in empty lots to rot and die in despair. Or as it was in certain Indian tribes in Alaska when in the dead of winter and food was scarce the older ones were left beside the trail for the bears to eat. The reasoning was that in the spring the Indians would hunt and kill and eat the bear thus affecting some sort of reunion with their dead parents and honoring everyone's spirit in the exchange. Modern adults no longer hunt and eat bears.

Today when parents are abandoned they often exhibit greater medical problems than their happier non abandoned counter parts. Depression is a major undiagnosed illness in nursing homes and among the abandoned. It is in fact an illness which defines older Americans especially if that parent is alone without a partner or spouse. Medical issues such as depression and especially depression form a convenient excuse for abandonment. Children say that it is just too difficult to deal with grandma's mental health when in fact it becomes an inescapable chain that traps the parent and the children into a non relational existence. American adult children, and I think most adult children, seem to believe that they are entitled to a perfect relationship with their parents and if it can't be perfect, if it is challenging in any way, then they are justified in abandonment because she/he is just too difficult to relate to.

Is this abandonment a natural occurrence in the evolution of humanity? Are we developing into a species that generates expendable human beings without thought of consequence? Is this an issue that should even be considered worthy of change and exposure?

TEMPTING EXPLANATIONS

There are two theories of how the estrangement between parents and adult children occurs outside of the Parental Alienation Syndrome of children during divorce. The first is that the adult child has fallen into a cult or more recently that a "cult" can exist between two people – husband and wife for example. The second is that parental abandonment is another aspect of domestic violence.

While it is quite tempting to make the connection between cultism and parental abandonment, the cult description does not quite fit all the dynamics of parental abandonment. The mind control manipulation techniques are similar but not completely explanatory. Cultism or being a member of a cult does not explain the animosity that develops against the parents without the presence of a religious community. In the abandonment of parents we find that the adult child seems to continue to interact with the real world of work and peer group involvement. There usually is an absence of the overtones of a political or religious support group who shares a common belief system. While spreading the lies about the parents is common among those who are in relationship with the adult child and the third party intervener, it does not rise to a cult mind control central thesis or belief system. The lies and vilification of the parents tend to be more in the order of an explanation as to why the parents of the adult child are not in the picture. Sometimes the side benefit of sympathy for the "abused child" is another side benefit. In some cases the lies and vilification of the parents may be used as an explanation for why the daughter or son in law has "married beneath them" or why that person doesn't quite measure up to the ideal mate. He was abused as a child suggests that he has undiscovered potential and will develop into that ideal mate.

While there are cults that have mind control techniques designed to cause the inductee to commit sometimes violent acts, those conditions are just absent in the majority of reported cases of abandonment of parents.

CAUSES OF ABANDONMENT AND ALIENATION FROM PARENTS

There are no known studies of the phenomenon that has been described in these chapters but again observations, experiences and narratives demonstrate these eight general categories of causation in no particular order of importance or prevalence. It is also important when reading through these cause categories to remember that there may be and probably is a mixing of several causal factors.

Cause No 1 - A Simple Breakdown

The simple breakdown of close relationships in a modern society that has seen the failure of attachment in many areas of our lives: extended family influence, the valuing of busyness of work and the consumption of time and the growing geographic distances between families are but a few of the contributing influences in estrangement. And these simple breakdowns in the relationship between parent and adult child can occur more easily than parents can imagine. The parent/child relationship requires as much care and time investment as any other valuable relationship in our lives. Some of us have been led to believe in the magic of our connection with our child and that there is an unbreakable bond, probably biological, that will sustain it forever. This is probably not the case. When geographic distance occurs because of jobs or other reasons, communication becomes less and less. Simple details of daily living are summarized which limit the meaningfulness of communication. Slowly the weekly telephone calls become less meaningful arriving at a perfunctory recitation of what the week or month has brought to the adult child or the parent. Long distant holiday sharing becomes more tense and expensive as children come along. And those short-term holidays exaggerate trivial disagreements and misunderstandings that families always have. Adding those things all together avoidance becomes tempting to the adult child. At the same time more and more meaning is placed on holidays by aging parents partly because they realize that there are fewer to share and because secretly they believe adult children have an obligation to come. Sooner or later the adult child has competing influences on where to spend holidays. And so it goes...

Families who have been separated by distance also lose the ability to cope with family disputes and irritations. In the extended families of years ago family members were forced to find ways of ignoring, coping or resolving family disputes and irritants because of the necessities associated with survival as well as community values but also by the simple fact they saw each other every day. Now days when families come together once a year or less the normal family irritants are exaggerated and unresolved because simply everyone has forgotten how to resolve them.

As a result, families drift apart and soon the weekly phone calls become monthly phone calls until what is unspoken is the pain of abandonment as parents sit in their homes waiting for that perfunctory birthday or Mothers day call that may or may not come. Parents do not lose their historical thinking about their children. They remember them as little guys and girls sitting on their laps happy and contented. And it probably is correct to say parents live in the past in terms of their feelings, memories and expectations about their children. And so they are injured when their adult children change who they are, their values and when they lose or moderate their connections to the past and to them. Adult children have no clue generally as to the consequence of their decisions on their parents. They just don't think about it or value the results of their decisions on the lives of their parents.

Parents must carefully and thoughtfully plan how they will maintain their relationship with their adult children including scheduled visits to them. They may even consider a move to the city or area the children now reside. Distance in itself calls for affirmative action on the part of the parents and the adult children to take seriously the continuation of their relationship. This is especially true for those adult children with young families as they become more and more limited in their ability to communicate and invest in their own parents needs.

In their book *The Lonely American,* Dr. Jacqueline Olds focuses on the interaction between social forces and individual psychology. Many of the stories are about feeling left out, an experience that seems easy to dismiss as trivial or even childish but an emerging understanding of the feeling of being left out helps to make sense of its central role as an engine of human emotion and behavior. Adding to this is the recent publication and research of Dr. John Caccioppo from the University of Chicago whose research finds a significant link between mortality in seniors and loneliness. Feelings of loneliness and being left out give rise to issues of depression and anxiety disorders. No one is able to relate when trapped in the depths of depression.

The bottom-line here is that the parent/adult child relationship is much more fragile than we, as parents or children, have been led to believe. It is held together in large part by social norms and in today's world these are changing rapidly. With that change, comes a loss of information about behavior, loyalty, belonging, getting along and values with the unavoidable consequence of estrangement.

Cause No. 2 Third Party Interveners

The negative influence of 3rd parties on the relationship between parents and their adult children is by far the most prevalent cause of abandonment and estrangement. These 3rd parties include daughters and sons in law, the family of the person your child married into, some peer relationships, cult type leaders, particularly those in religious institutions. Often the persons who marry your children find it desirable to get rid of you and find effective ways to do it. They blame their spouse's parents for behavior in their spouse they would like to manipulate or change. Others demand the complete devotion/attention/affection of their partner in order to fill their own emptiness. If the adult child is "attached" to his/her parents the spouse sees that as a withholding from them of total commitment. Another motivation is the person your adult child marries is hell bent on a building a successful family (in their narcissistic image) and that means no interference from anyone is tolerated or even the possibility of interference.

No less serious is when your adult child marries or commits to an abusive spouse, a narcissistic or sociopathic spouse. The first thing the abuser seeks to do is separate your child from his/her family or significant others who the abuser sees as a person likely to interfere in an abusive relationship or who is aware and likely to identify the true nature of that abuser. The next thing, of course, is to increase the abuse in severity and frequency.

Another real motivation for a third party in law to alienate their spouse's parents, or their own for that matter, is the need to limit their world. These adult children may have emotional or mental issues, often born of an anxiety disorder, and their need to limit the influences and dynamics of their world to only what they can manage, or perhaps control, so they define parents as uncontrollable so they can keep their peaceful existence. You hear them say "Your mother is too controlling."

In particular, the very real consequences of parental alienation (PAS) and targeted parents or the presences of malevolent narcissists in the family unit who target both or individual parents cause unimaginable losses. Sometimes during a divorce particularly traumatizing divorce lawyers can deliberately cause irretrievable alienation for their own self-serving financial interests. A simple internet search of Parental Alienation Disorder will bring many websites up that will inform you about PAS and the alienation of a parent by the other parent in divorce circumstances. Thankfully the world is now taking this seriously after the initial work of Richard a. Gardner, MD in "The Parental Alienation Syndrome". A good study of what happens to these adult children who have been alienated from a parent is "adult children of parental alienation syndrome: breaking the ties that bind" by Amy J.L. Baker. Additionally for those who encounter a particularly chilling 3rd party personality read "The Lucifer Effect" by Philip Zimbardo.

Third parties who practice alienation are vulnerable in one way and that is they fear exposure. They operate in secret and cannot tolerate the idea of the public learning about who they really are. From the simplest confrontation to full blown police interference their behaviors are either diminished or exaggerated by their fear of exposure.

Who are these third parties?

They are people who have at their core a belief system that justifies the damage done to their spouses, their children, friends and their families. They can be, among other things, personality oriented toward narcissistic or sociopathic tendencies or outright mentally ill. All of these tendencies are present in some degree in the person that marries into the targeted family. For sure third parties are not empathic. They are capable of avoiding or diminishing or not feeling the pain they are inflicting on others. Because of this lack of empathy they will continue to have discomfort with their own children and their spouses. They do not seek therapy as they are sure the angst in the family is someone else's fault. Read more about this in The Empathy Trap, a book, which demonstrates this issue very well.

The beginning of a marriage and the introduction of a third party into a new family system is fraught with tension and uncertainty. The new spouse (third party) is challenged with a new set of dynamics that they are unfamiliar with and ones which may or may not be to their liking. When those third party new spouses suffer from low self-esteem, narcissistic or sociopathic tendencies or an exaggerated need to dominate, the estrangement of the spouses' parents can be an avenue of resistance and a coping mechanism for their own short comings. For example, the third party may result in an over powering urge to dominate your adult child as a means to have all the attention directed toward themselves. Perhaps this is a way of working out insecurity, low self esteem, a fear of failing in the marriage or a need to legitimatize them in the relationship. All of these needs speak to the motivation to have no alternative voice, no competitive stories about the success or failures of the relationship, no competition for the affection of either the spouse or the children of the marriage and the elimination of influences they are not familiar with. Some of the new spouses can cause abandonment and rejection as a form of anxiety reduction. They are very insecure and anxiety- ridden people who need to limit their world and the players in it because they can't handle the "normal" anxiety produced by a family's interaction. It would be interesting to know if this is a pattern in the third party and if they also try to limit their world at work or socially to satisfy the same avoidance need.

Some third parties have strong needs for clarity and predictability in their lives. The fewer people to manage the easier their lives are. These third parties are lazy and generally immature and seek to avoid confusion and stress. They will seek to eliminate the families of their new spouse as well as his/her social friends putting the entire emphasis of social interaction on the third party's family and friends. Essentially the third party will seek to dissociate your adult child from all aspects of his historic social and familial life in favor of his/her own.

Anxiety ridden third parties are simply incapable of responding to the new dynamics brought on by the introduction to a new family. They are fear dominated often mildly paranoid and very needy people. They attribute nefarious motives and behaviors to the family of your adult child in order to avoid the consequences of their own fear based perceptions. These third parties are very good at convincing others of their perceptions because their very lives depend on avoiding the fear of people who might hurt them or expose them for who they really are as human beings.

Are they evil?

Sometimes they are evil. When the estrangement of the targeted parents is pleasure producing and the abuse of the estranged parents is prolonged without complete separation, when the targeted parents are "kept around" for a display of what is wrong with them, or to be useful monetarily or as babysitters, and hyper criticalness becomes commonplace, then yes they are evil. When the goal of the third parties' behavior is the perpetuation of human misery rather than as a side effect of another goal, then the third party is evil indeed.

However when the estrangement is complete almost immediately on the third parties entrance into the family unit, then they are probably not inherently evil. They are probably very disturbed but their goals are quite different. These third parties want dominance and blind loyalty directed to his/her own family unit. The proof of the loyalty required of your adult child is the complete abandonment of his/her family.

Parents of the third party and their contribution to the estrangement

At best the parents of the third party are co-conspirators either through their tolerance of the rejection of the targeted parents or fear of rejection themselves. One of the best communications that these third parties make is the clear messages that "if you rock the boat, defy me, you are expendable too". Often these third party parents have a history of alienation from their own parents. Hence their adult child and been brought up with the core beliefs required to completely reject the family of the new spouse.

There is also some evidence that there are "cult like families" who for generations target others in order to keep their own members in their group and make clear to outsiders what their fate will be should they defy the matriarch or patriarch of the group. These families have traceable rejections for as far back as can be remembered. The current matriarch didn't speak to her mother and her mother didn't speak to hers and the current matriarch's children marry only those women or men who will easily give up their own mothers. This outcome is usually dominated by early on labeling and defining of the targeted mother as mentally ill or socially unacceptable. The current cult like family is always self defined as "special" and "above the crowd" either though education, wealth or social status.

In most cases, the parents of the third party, who are not cult like or who are not co-conspirators, are ineffective at intervention at best. They will simply fail at any effort to correct the behavior of their child toward his/her spouse's parents. At this point then the third party's parents become apathetic and allow the cruelty to go on without protest. These parents have then taken on the historical position of allowing evil and cruelty to take place and have agreed to become a silent witness to this. There is pleasure giving in this position and one of the most evil of all evil behaviors – that of a condoner of cruelty.

Likewise siblings of either the third party or the targeted spouse are ineffective at reversing the abandonment. Some of the siblings are tolerated because they are perceived by the third party as lacking any ability to challenge them. Likewise some are rejected along with the targeted parents as being too aware of the third parties agenda of dominance and cruelty.

Who is to blame?

Clearly and without a doubt your adult child is to blame. Whatever mind altering techniques employed by a third party to an adult child, on some level, usually overt, the adult child agrees to abandon his/her parents and to stand by and watch them suffer excruciating pain. These adult children do not change their minds, they reject verbally and by avoidance all efforts to communicate with their parents or to problem solve with them. There is no evidence of a struggle or any confusion on the part of your adult child that is communicated to the targeted parents. As well there is a complete rejection of any efforts by friends and other family members "to work it out" or "to be a go between". Often your adult child will not only go along with the intervener but participate by behaving hatefully him or herself.

For those adult children who keep their parents around and prolong the obvious signs of abandonment, they are participatory in the torture of their parents, knowing the extent of the pain being caused to them; they use their special knowledge of their parents to drive the knife in further. These adult children, who keep their parents around, sometimes to baby-sit or to lend them money, have already psychologically abandoned them. Their goal is to prolong the pain and misery as long as possible and for only as long as it benefits them.

Clearly and without a doubt the second group of people who are to blame are those around the adult child and the third party who fail to speak up and fail to employ ancient and well-tested penalties for abandoning a parent and who keep the secret of abandonment from the rest of the world. They are apathetic or worse fearful of their own loses. They "cave in" to emotional blackmail. Often, quite pathetically, these third party enablers are therapists or clergy.

Ill Treatment of parents is contagious

A good many parents who have experienced ill treatment, estrangement or abandonment by an adult child are also ill treated, abandoned or estranged by their other adult children later on. It is contagious. The pattern is that one follows another one and it doesn't necessarily follow birth order. Dialogue with adult children who have core beliefs that their parents are wrong, abusive, or deserving of alienation is very persuasive dialogue and these brain washing techniques work about half the time.

What are the chances that abandonment will be reversed?

Third parties "install" a core belief in their victim spouses, which among other things redefines the ethical and moral teaching of the entire society – to honor your parents. It is frighteningly successful. The longer that core belief is held and unchallenged the less the chances of reconciliation with the adult child's parents. One of the clear signs that an adult child has been brain washed is when they are claiming their parents were abusive but are totally unable to testify to any treatment significant enough to support that conclusion. In fact many adult children so brainwashed or gas lighted cannot recall any good events of their childhood.

What are the chances these core beliefs will carry over to the grandchildren?

Unfortunately these beliefs will carry over into grandchildren as well. Grandchildren are no more immune from the third party's goal of estrangement than their parent is immune. And the grandchildren will grow up without an image or a relationship with the abandoned parents. They will not be able to recognize you even as a stranger. There is a particular kind of hate that causes adult children to hate their parents more than they love their children in denying them their generational benefits of family.

What, if anything, can be done to avoid being the targeted parent?

Often, the initial reaction to the first inklings of estrangement is missed by the targeted parents, because they are so eager to make a good impression and to have this new family member like them. If the clues aren't missed they are defined away as a little strange behavior but the targets don't want to have a "bad scene" so they brush over it. When the targeted parents finally are moved to speak out they generally approach the adult child in the absence of the third party. That seems very normal to them as they don't yet have a relationship with the third party and don't want to offend him or her or cause "trouble". Bad mistake however, as this is taken as an opportunity by the third party to illustrate how the targeted parents are attempting to "interfere" in the marriage. When the targeted parents finally figure out they are being sidelined or abandoned they grieve openly, cry, and plead for explanations. The more emotional those behaviors are the more ammunition is given to the third party to define them as "mentally ill", "crazy" or "devious". So the obvious answer is to try and be alert whenever there is a life-changing event about to occur in your family. Be alert and do not ever behave in a way that reinforces the image the third party is drawing. If the third party is defining you as interfering do not ever offer an opinion about anything. Most importantly do not be emotional at any time. And if you feel that you need to challenge the behaviors of "being left out", and then calmly have a meeting with both your adult child and the third party and attempt to make a deal with a set schedule of involvement. Constantly kiss the third party's butt in other words.

The alternative answer to what can you do is to set boundaries early in the relationship and gently confront early signs of estrangement. Involve the third party's parents and siblings. No not avoid gentle conflict management. It has to be an individual decision when the stakes are so high. Look at Judy Ringer's work on "How to have difficult conversations."

Also at the beginning of the estrangement you might ask a family friend or someone known to both of you to intervene and to express the concern that you have regarding involvement with your adult child and his family. Be always careful to refer to them as a family unit so the third party cannot claim to be left out.

If these things fail, and they probably will, then resign yourself to your abandonment and continue to hope that one day your adult child will realize what he or she has become. The likelihood of that happening is beyond the pale of this book and to horrible to speak out loud.

What do third parties react to?

The only thing a third party fears is exposure to the public of less than admirable behavior. That would also include "cult families". For this reason the third party will more than likely begin immediately to disparage the targeted parents as mentally ill or socially unacceptable or interfering or dominating. So by the time you are ready to expose them it is too late and the best you can do is defend yourself. When the third party is a religious organization or the offending spouse is fully emerged in a religious organization he/she will be given much support from other church members so be particularly careful and chose your words carefully. One way is to join the religious organization yourself and be a model member so the third party is disarmed from painting a nasty picture of you. Very difficult to do however.

Cause No. 3 The Dynamics of Emotional Disarray

The dynamics of emotional disarray, mental illness especially depression, addiction on the part of the parents or the adult children, and serious or chronic illness including general disabilities associated with aging.

Lumping all of these social ills into one category may seem a bit of a general sweep and it is, but for the purposes of the parent/adult child relationship they can all have the same effect. The dynamic of these social ills have a direct and chronically sad destructive effect on the relationship between parent and child in that these ills take the primary focus off the relationship and on to something extraneous and powerful. The relationship becomes secondary to the illness or the addictions. Often the illness causes a leper like effect in the relationship where the adult child and/or the parent intuitively shuns the other. Shunning in this situation is greatly approved by the general public and peer groups. Very sad. But if someone asks at the cocktail party about your mother and you reply that she is mentally ill. The comment back is "I am so sorry" and the conversation moves immediately onto another topic.

Depression, anxiety disorders and severe mental illness cause breaches in all relationships. That is the work of mental illness – to isolate the sufferer. When our children are beaten down with depression or terrified by anxiety, their relationships with others simply takes too much energy. Relationships require a normalcy that they mostly cannot muster on a sustained basis. One study indicates that mothers who exhibit chronic depression are more likely to be abandoned by their children. The why of that is unknown? Another study indicates that when a mother has long term depression the brains of their growing children are affected and do not develop normally.

Another little explored area is that of a child who is diagnosed with Oppositional Defiant Disorder, sometimes associated with particularly nasty divorces. This childhood emotional illness may be the result of the impact of divorce on children and consequently on the estrangement of parents. This connection may be closely tied together. However, it doesn't really matter whether the illness is on the part of the child or the parent. Estrangement occurs historically. The mental health systems in most countries and certainly mass media do little to assist the family members of mental illness sufferers to learn new behaviors to continue those relationships with boundaries if necessary. It is heartbreaking when a child or a parent suffers from severe mental illness such that makes "living together" dangerous or unbearable. But does complete severance of the relationship need happen or through education and assistance can there be some meaningful relationship continued. Clearly the presence and support of family members are a major component for recovery of most illnesses – mental, emotional, physical or addictive. How sad that we take the first exit away from an ill parent or child.

Most of the adult children who abandoned their parents commonly accuse their parent of being "mentally ill". The majority of those accusations is false and serves a very evil purpose: that is to find a good excuse for the abandonment in order to avoid any social criticism. These adult children find an easy out in the accusation of mental illness toward their parents. After all, who would blame an adult child for severing relationships with his/her parents if they are mentally ill? The mentally ill are the modern day lepers. In this accusation there is a tone of contagion and like a leper the adult children are admired and soothed by their peers for chasing these sick parents to the outskirts of the village and disassociating any care for their well being.

When those accusations are not false, when the parent is suffering from some form of mental illness, those parents need their familial relationships even more for healing, for encouragement to stick with treatment and medication and for companionship. Even though the mental health profession is silent on the issue it is a question whether it is possible for a mentally ill parent to heal and recover when their adult children abandon them and when they do not have the support of loving family. There are many options for maintaining relationships with parents who suffer mental illness and only as an absolute last resort should a parental relationship be abandoned.

"I have recently made up my mind that I have lost the battle of ever reconciling with my daughter. The 2 times I have once sent a loving card expressing that I was sorry if I ever hurt/upset her & the other time I rang her; both times she filed for a court order preventing me from making any kind of contact because I have mental illness (cause by family member's abuse when I was growing up) & now I just feel that the hurt I keep enduring from trying to reconcile in a healthy way is just causing me more grief. I will move on with my life & find what happiness I can. I miss her soft skin against my cheek & her warm embrace, which came so easy to her & I. Now I feel the emptiness, numbness, despair & disbelief of once was an awesome relationship... just such a waste. But if I deal on the ifs & buts, I will destroy myself with my thoughts & I have been given a life & live it to the fullest is what is my plan. I can change my thought process but nobody else's thoughts & feelings".

Clearly depression and anxiety are either the cause of estrangement or obvious consequences of it. These two particular factors seem to be present in a majority of the cases.

Addiction is another horrible social ill that severs relationships between adult children and parents with little regard to which side is addicted. Fortunately there is a very helpful system of help for family members of addicts called Al anon. Al anon has a system for assisting, educating and supporting family members of addicts, which has found success over a good many years. Boundary setting with addicts is very important and behaviors like that must be learned, taught by experts and those resources are out there for both parents of addicts and for adult children who are addicts.

Cause No. 4 Traumatic Events

The occurrence of a traumatic event such as the death of one of the parents, a public humiliation, or a sudden negative experience perceived as such by the child. Here it is convenient for us to make a distinction between traumas. There are those traumas such a terminal illness or a car accident that are not subject to blame and harsh judgment. Then there are those that do lend themselves to blame and judgment such as an affair that becomes public, a criminal charge against a parent, drug usage, sexual misconduct, an traffic accident by a drunk driver, etc. One expects the family to rally around the ill parent or a surviving spouse in the case of blameless trauma. However when a blame trauma occurs there are no social norms dictating behavior, the child is left to make judgments unaided by social norms and must rely heavily on the influence of those around him/her. One thinks about Chelsea Clinton who became the peacemaker during the sexual scandal in the White House.

It makes a big difference if the parent is killed in a car accident because of drunkenness or because the road was icy. The child, adult or not, will be faced with a very different trauma, a very different peer group reaction and a very different media reaction. The consequences of the trauma to the family's social standing, job stability and peer group reaction will all impact the relationship between parent and child.

The role of mass media involvement in these traumas cannot be underestimated. When the media jumps on a story and spins it as a judgmental one, the child, adult or not, is instantly conflicted and must sometimes chose between peer relationships and parental ones. We are all aware of Bernie

Madoff and the effect his public crime had on his son who committed suicide.

These traumatic events can also be the sudden death of a parent when the effect on the child is so severe that he/she needs to blame the surviving parent. Sometimes the parent or the child simply shuts down emotionally and is unable to continue a bond emotionally with the other.

There are some reports of a parent convicted of a crime and the children of that parent abandoning them. Certainly these traumatic events can cause severe trauma to a family unit and when the trauma is so out of the range of normative behavior it can be very destructive. Here we might think of the very normal life of a secretary who is suddenly discovered to have been embellishing her employer for years. Not only is his/her reputation and public and private image shattered so also are the offspring of the person accused.

Cause No. 5 The Dependency of Elderly Parents

The growing dependency of aging parents and the social and cultural demands made on an already overburdened adult child both emotionally and financially are often cause for abandonment. Certainly the availability of alternative care such as nursing homes almost encourages the abandonment or estrangement. There is a growing body of material generally categorized as elder abuse which is all enlightening as to the relationships between parents and adult children. This area is one where the greatest amount of physical violence occurs as well as complete abandonment. Perhaps it is a primal, intuitive and reptilian brain response to that which is aged or diseased. We avoid what stinks, what is weak. Animals are driven out of the pack or herd when they can't cut it anymore. And then there is the ever present need in the human spirit for a scapegoat. The oldest of remedies for our angst is to blame and persecute others. It makes us feel better. Anyone that has ever worked in a nursing home is a good source of information regarding the common abandonment of the elderly.

Aging parents and the social and cultural demands made on an already overburdened adult child both emotionally and financially are commonly the last straw in terms of pressure on the adult child coupled with the absence of cultural norms and expectations for coping. Even if these relationships have been "limping along" throughout the years of adulthood in their child, the dependant parent becomes even less available to their children and a relationship with them.

It is fair to say that adults who reside in nursing homes or assisted living facilities are hardly ever visited by their adult children. Of course there are exceptions but those exceptions are usually when the parents and the children live in the same community and an occasional but short visit doesn't place too much of a burden on the adult child.

Interestingly enough, those government agencies coupled with researchers on elderly health tip toe around the issue of abandonment by adult children and the impact on their emotional and physical health. Research papers and official pamphlets name "isolation" and "neglect" and "ignoring" as forms of abuse. But they all stop short of naming who is doing that to the elderly. They make statements like "50% of all nursing home residents do not have close relatives" but there is little beyond those statements as to why or who is doing this neglect or the impact on the wellbeing of the patient.

Frankly, I believe the literature is hovering toward labeling the abandonment of the elderly by the adult children as neglect. However in doing so serious legal and social issues arise with that naming. Is abandonment actionable at law? What should/can be public policy for adult child abandonment of their parents?

Clearly the abandonment, isolation and shunning of the elderly by their adult children is emotional abuse and that is the best you can say about it. Put Mom or Dad in a nursing home, visit a couple of times a year for an hour or so, call the head nurse every couple of months and call it caring so as to avoid the label of neglect and abuse? Notice that all the behaviors listed above are typical of the adult children whose parents are in nursing homes and we all want to call that ok. After all there isn't much to talk about anymore is there?

Cause No. 6 Failed Adult Children

Failed Children are here in defined as adult children who have not achieved maturity and who cannot, for one reason or the other, conduct themselves in a responsible manner. They do not have a defined philosophy out of which they measure their behavior as good or bad. They are not involved in nor are they capable of meaningful and non-abusive relationships with a significant other including relationships with friends and their parents in some way consistent with the traditions associated with cultural and generational norms. These adult children often have tremendously traumatic lives and the parents are often caught up in a constant and ongoing drama of attempts to "fix" them. These relationships are marked with a pattern of dependency and false obligatory ideas of closeness. They are adult children who are addicts, ne'er-do-wells, can't hold a job or maintain a relationship, pay child support or manage money.

The parent/adult child relationship in this category is somewhat of a hybrid wherein the adult child gives only the illusion of connection. The connection is fairly predatory because these adult children use their parents for support and money and will continue this usage until there is nothing left of the parent's financial stability. It doesn't matter if that financial support is termed a loan as it is never paid back beyond a couple of token efforts. On top of the monetary drain there is a constant level of worry placed upon the parents by these adult children that drains energy and joy from their lives. The tales of hard times: "I am getting evicted because I can't pay the rent. I am out of work because I got fired. I am going to jail for failure to pay child support. I owe someone money to pay a gambling debt." The list goes on and the stories go on until the worry of the parents becomes a daily activity, depression sets in and the parents are so financially strapped they can't pay their own bills. Many times these parents will have co-signed personal loans for the adult child or used their house as collateral for a loan that will never be paid by the child.

"Financial abuse is often the motivator for beating up Grandpa or neglecting Mom," says Kathleen Quinn, executive director of the National Adult Protective Services Association, which represents state and local programs that investigate abuse of vulnerable adults and takes steps to protect the victims. Ninety percent of abusers are family members or trusted others. Of all reported elder-abuse cases, financial exploitation is reported most frequently. The referrals we get run the gamut, from someone having their Social Security check being taken to an account drained of over $200,000."

Frequently these monetary betrayals turn into elder abuse of neglect or physical abuse. The elder parents become isolated and depressed and worried into emotional trauma so they become more isolated and more vulnerable to the aggression of the adult child and much less able to defend themselves.

A very public example of this was the Brooke Astor case helped raise awareness of elder financial abuse. The New York Post called it the "swindle trial." Jurors likened it to a "Shakespearean tragedy." When New York socialite Anthony D. Marshall was convicted of defrauding and stealing from his elderly mother, philanthropist Brooke Astor, reports detailed how he conspired with lawyer Francis Morrissey to amend her will in his favor, took millions without her consent, and lifted paintings from her walls while she languished in her Park Avenue home eating oatmeal.

Elder financial abuse is "the ultimate betrayal," says Colleen Toy White, a superior court judge in Ventura County,

California, who sees roughly 40 cases of such abuse each month. "It's shocking to see how vulnerable the elder person is."

Cause No. 7 Unresolved Generational Trauma

Generational trauma unresolved and active within the family dynamics of the parents and the adult children is a very real but often neglected exploration of why adult children leave their parents. "Sometimes, we reject or distance ourselves from our parents in an attempt to feel free. Yet that only causes more suffering. The path toward true peace is to make peace with our parents, even if they are deceased" according to the Hellinger Institute whose work is directed toward the issue of generational trauma.

How does this work? Who knows? But there is clear evidence that trauma unresolved as recent history or as far back as 3 generations is present, active and destructive in the lives of parent and adult children today. There is evidence of ostracizing almost cult like families that for several generations in a row men and women that marry into them are "required", mostly nonverbally, to abandon their own parents and do so. The conversations active within these ostracizing families are open, often stated as a kind of anthem with happy overtones about not seeing their own parents for years.

The Hellinger Institute in southern California has led the way into an investigation of generational trauma. "Children seldom or never dare to live a happier or more fulfilling life than their parents. Unconsciously they remain loyal to unspoken family traditions that work invisibly. Family constellations are a way of discovering underlying family bonds and forces that have been carried unconsciously over several generations." Bert Hellinger, the founder of this work, and Mark Wolynn, who is the director, have studied and treated families for more than 50 years, observed that many of us unconsciously "take on" destructive familial patterns of anxiety, depression, anger, guilt, aloneness, alcoholism and even illness as a way of "belonging" in our families. Bonded by a deep love, a child will often sacrifice his own best interests in a vain attempt to ease the suffering of a parent or other family member. In unpacking these histories, the process examines the tragic events in war? Who died in or participated in the holocaust? Who profited from another's loss? Who was wrongly accused? Who was jailed or institutionalized? Who had a physical, emotional or mental disability? Who had a significant relationship prior to getting married, and what happened? Who experienced an early trauma which now affects us and our children?

Looking back three generations, we ask: Who died early? Who left? Who was abandoned, isolated or excluded from the family? Who was adopted or who gave a child up for adoption? Who died in childbirth? Who was murdered or murdered someone? Who committed suicide? Who suffered separation from a mother? And so on. Most importantly, we see how tragic events have deeply impacted our families. We see how our parents and grandparents struggled. We ask: Are we struggling similarly? The imprint of these events can become the blueprint for future generations.

Even when children distance themselves from their families, they tend to feel little relief from the symptoms of anxiety, depression or lostness. Much of our suffering comes from a deep loyalty to our parents and families. In an innocent way, we imagine that we can somehow alleviate the family unhappiness by sharing it. But this fantasized thinking only leads to more unhappiness. Sometimes, we reject or distance ourselves from our parents in an attempt to feel free. Yet that only causes more suffering. The path toward true peace is to make peace with our parents, even if they are deceased. This work makes that possible.

What's unresolved with our parents does not automatically disappear. It serves as a template that forges our later relationships. The work of the Hellinger Institute is ongoing and promises to bring more and more enlightenment into the issues of family relationships.

I am sorry to say that the pain was so great that I tried to take my life. As I laid in the ER in which I only made by less than 5 minutes, my daughter was called and advised I flat lined and on the 8th call her husband answered her cell and said she's not there. I think of suicide all the time because at one time I had what I thought to be a great relationship with my daughter. In getting so sick (emotional pain, etc) I have alienated my whole family because let's face it who wants to be around someone that was crying all the time. I know suicide is not the answer but sometimes, like you said, it seems it's the only thing that will stop the pain. It took more than 2 years for me to have some form of healing. Went back to school at the age of 55 and eventually heard from my daughter when she was in midst of divorce. Then BAM! she found a boyfriend and once again I said the wrong thing and I have been cut off again. I am so sorry that she made that initial contact with me again because it set me so far back. The funny thing is, I put her through college with no student loans (paid for everything) and the kicker is she has masters in psychology. She knows that I was abandoned by my own mother (with abandonment issues of my own) and she was the last person on this earth that I ever thought would abandon me! Every day I try and keep myself busy from the time I wake up until the time I go to sleep just not to think of her. Anyone that thinks us abandoned parents have no thoughts of suicide is wrong or misinformed. I wish all these parents heartfelt sympathy and definitely have empathy. God Bless each and every one of us. I have endured some tough times in life but never like this. I worked 10-12 hour days so she would not want for anything (I was extremely poor growing up as a child) and I did all myself for her without any help from her father. All she thinks about is the negative. I said to her "can't you seem to think of all the good things we had between us?" but that is an area that she does not want to visit. So now I am estranged from my family which I love very much but I can't say I blame them because I was a mess when she cut me off without any rhyme or reason and I still don't know what I've done. At least if I knew I could possibly try and talk about it but she refuses to give me a reason. She had me arrested 3 times when I tried to call her for harassment so my therapist said she was a threat to my freedom and I should not try and contact her anymore and I won't. I find solace in these pages and the wonderful articles about the phenomenon of this abandonment. I still envy my neighbors when I see their children and grandchildren visit every week and remember how my daughter drove 2 hours every week to see me and then got married and all of a sudden forgot about me. Blocked my number from her phone...I could go on and on. Suicide is not the answer as one therapist said to me "if she doesn't care about you now, she won't care if you're dead". Made sense. But anyone this page may seem to help in saving a life is well worth it. Please don't give up posting that because we all need help...some more than others. Thanks for listening.

Cause No. 8 A Flawed Match

That is to say that the personalities don't mesh. They may not simply have anything in common. There is no energy between them. The parents and the adult child, as that child has evolved, have no affinity for each other. They are not kindred spirits. There has been a failure of long term bonding. This is called Attachment Theory and promotes the idea that there are negative consequences when the parent/child bond is not established. One of those consequences is that the adult child is rather a "stranger" to the parent and vice versa.

This cause is a bit hard to grasp although it has been fairly common. A parent who realizes that a child is homosexual and cannot accept this child is an example. A parent who has a child with a birth defect or mentally challenged in some way can feel a sense of rejection of the child at some emotional or psychological level. The result in these examples is that bonding does not occur, or is damaged in some way. Then the parent and child become as mere acquaintances to each other.

Another example is a child who just hears a different drummer, can't wait to grow up and move on. And they do just that. There are no issues or animosity or bad behavior on either part. They just don't click and have nothing to talk about.

Attachment theory of child development would speak to behaviors consistent with a failure of nurturing from birth to 18 months or to changes that might occur in the mid teens. For our purposes however, something in the relationship doesn't gel and beyond mere politeness there is no relationship which can and usually does lead to a separation, at least psychologically, between the adult child and the parent.

I feel like a worthless "thing" sometimes, less than human... I must have been, and am, such an awful, awful person in her eyes that she can just throw me away like trash...I came to the unpleasant conclusion that my own child just plain *doesn't like me* as a person. I annoy her, and everything I am, and everything I do is just all *wrong*. My entire personality is flawed, in her estimation. Whatever it is she wanted me to be, or whatever kind of mother she expected me to be, I was *not*. Sad to say that she was secretly my favorite of my 4 daughters, and we were so close at one time... My very existence seems to be an affront to my own child. I don't feel very good about myself right now, and if I didn't have my faith, I'm afraid of what I might do... I am fighting depression and despair with every bit of feeble strength I have left.

The Injury

Frozen grief, frozen sadness and ambiguous loss are often the terms used to describe the ongoing grieving state of the abandoned parent – a grief state which feels unmanageable. But even those terms hardly describes the deep soul breaking pain that abandonment by your own children can bring. The pain is fundamental, experienced on a cellular level and imagined as beyond that which can be borne. Many of these abandoned parents harbor suicidal thoughts out of proportion to that of the general population. Some estimates put that ratio at 2 out of 3 who admit thinking that their pain is so great and hope is so lost that dying is the only remedy. Studies also show that grieving is more often the cause of suicide than depression. It may be that these suicidal thoughts are actually those messengered to them by their adult children who either process them as dead or wish they were. The CDC lists depression and loneliness as leading causes of suicide among older citizens. Loneliness also shortens life span and contributes too many physical and mental illnesses.

These parents experience brutal and acidic pain every day of their lives and for some this covers a span of 15 to 20 years. The question of why abandoned parents cannot or do not heal is very complex involving nearly all aspects of human life as we know it. In trying to understand and to find a balm for this pain, first let's look at the definition of family with apologies to social scientists who spend their lives trying to capture this concept.

Family is the essential societal unit. It function, historically, is to provide for the procreation of the human race by the birth, nurture and protection of the young. It houses and provides the essential "place" for humans to group themselves for protection and sustenance according to each person's usefulness.

More than that it provides the essential identity of each person: ideals, values, rituals, traditions, stories, history, attitudes, beliefs, family strength, family satisfaction, care taking of the infirm and elderly, stability, finances, a sense of family history, family roots. Family defines boundaries for what is acceptable and not acceptable both from the outside world and from the dynamics of life in a small unit. Family tells us what to do in almost every imaginable circumstance.

So image what happens to a human being when these identifiers are removed by abandonment. The parent finds themselves with no identity, wiped and erased are the rituals of holidays, enjoyment of shared ritual food, ideals and ethical constraints crushed, all possibilities of support for future events and the embarrassment of historical expectations unfulfilled. The abandonment by adult children removes from the parent all sense of psychological, social, spiritual well being, and identity. If I am not a mother who am I. This didn't happen to my mother or to anyone I know.

Abandonment leaves the parent outside the bounds of history. No one ever prepared the parent for this scenario. Preparation for future disaster is an essential part of family learning. What to do in the case of drought, bankruptcy, job loss and death is learned from our ancestors. It is family lore, stories of what was done when Uncle Bill died, how everyone survived the depression and victory gardens and when the lightning struck the cherry tree. No one ever dreamed of being abandoned by their children. So there is no "story" to be told that gives abandonment perspective or wisdom to be shared or to give the aggrieved and hurting a place to stop the pain and start healing. It has to be made up along the way.

Added to the mere fact of abandonment is the cruelty with which the act is sometimes performed. By observation and stories, we know that the abandonment is cruel, often accompanied by accusatorial, demeaning, harsh and abusive comments, wishes for the death of the parent and the withholding of the grandchildren, libelous and public accusations and most always with a blood chilling indifference. It is as if the adult children have pronounced the parent dead and they move on without them, justifying their actions by a complete deadening of reality. It is a hate crime and violent abuse of the worst order.

All of this produces a sense of humiliation and shame within the parents which, for many, is the first time in their lives they have experienced these feelings at least at the intensity which they experience it in abandonment. A leading researcher on humiliation, Dr. Evelin Lindner, defines humiliation as "the enforced lowering of a person or group, a process of subjugation that damages or strips away their pride, honor or dignity." Further, humiliation means to be placed, against ones will, in a situation where one is made to feel inferior. "One of the defining characteristics of humiliation as a process is that the victim is forced into passivity, acted upon, made helpless." Johan Galtung, a leading practitioner, agrees with Lindner that the infliction of humiliation is a profoundly violent psychological act that leaves the victim with a deep wound to the psyche.

So the "injury" to the parents as a result of the abandonment is to be stripped of all known familial defenses and resources and to be placed in an emotional circumstance of desolation and grief. Added to that are the very observable physical damages to the body of the parents often leading to disease and mental distress.

The abandonment by an adult child of the parent is very different than when a child dies because that abandoning child is still "out there" somewhere and consequently, the possibility of hope exists for reconciliation. We all live with the parable of the prodigal son. Unlike death, which is a closed door and invites a turning away, abandonment makes hope an enemy. Abandonment prevents closure and tantalizes the with a dream that is unrealistic and scarring. So, like blind people, who find themselves walking in four lane traffic at rush hour, they are confused, terrified and unable to find safety.

Dear......, everything you wrote here I could have written too! I couldn't imagine living without her, it hurt so deeply made me think I was a terrible person, must be true if she said so, we were so close. Then I just wanted to die not only because she left but how she left. Even when professional deemed her accusations "unfounded" and that she was mentally ill I still questioned myself? Thought less of myself. She once had so much power over me. Then it came to me, it is all about how she feels about herself spewed at me. That was 15 years ago. She still stays connected to me through her assaults; I haven't seen her since 1998. You are not alone! All those feelings of despair you have are normal with this kind of loss. The last thing you want to do is hurt yourself because believe me she won't come running back. More than likely it will be "see I told you she was crazy." talk to someone use therapy or medication or whatever you need to get through this. I have experienced a lot in my life and this has been the hardest thing of all. Sending hugs and angels your way!

Reasons why recovery is difficult

What is presented here is an attempt to identify the reasons why abandoned parents find healing so elusive and why they are unable, in many cases to move on with their lives or have years of struggle to regain their footing. For the abandoned parent it is nearly impossible to comprehend their children's intentional act of abandonment. The constant reviewing of history trying to understand what they did "wrong" coupled with shame and guilt make it nearly impossible, to get over it or move on. The abandonment coupled with the attitude of the adult child negates any historical concept of forgiveness rendering that spiritual tool useless and empty. Listed below are some common reasons why healing is elusive:

1. The act of abandonment itself is intentional and without regard to the cruelty of its consequences. During a telephone call to an adult daughter to say that the mother has cancer and is facing a dangerous surgery. The daughter says "Good Luck with that" and hangs up the phone. The stories are plentiful and range from sarcasm to denigration at such a level that one surmises that the adult child would not use such demeaning and vicious language to anyone ever again in their lifetime. However they seem to think it perfectly permissible to do so with an estranged parent. With most of these stories there seems to be an element of sadism: a smile on the face of the accusatorial son while witnessing the parent devastated; a sharing of the cruel actions with others while laughing and congratulating themselves on the separation. According to Science Daily, "Everyday sadists take pleasure in others' pain", Sept 12, 2013, Association for Psychological Science, "Most of the time, we try to avoid inflicting pain on others -- when we do hurt someone, we typically experience guilt, remorse, or other feelings of distress. But for some, cruelty can be pleasurable, even exciting." According to new research, this kind of everyday sadism is real and more

common than we might think. These adult children seem to have an inevitable need to find relationships and memberships in groups that practice this cruelty. Most people do not experience the intensity of hatred that adult children are capable of and exercise with no apparent remorse and hence the knife cuts all the deeper.

2. The act is beyond any concept of normalcy. Firmly implanted in the modern human mind is the idea of family and even though that concept has been expanded to include single parents, adoptive parents, same sex parents, it is still the essential unit by which we identify. We may grow up to reject the concept in favor of a more isolationist way of life but the "normal" is the family unit. Accompanying this concept of family is the notion of transition. Parents have children, children grow up, parent's age and die and all of this contained in the notion of essential unit in which we all find our being. Hating parents, abandoning parents and cruelty towards parents is not normally thought of as being within this tradition. Hence, there are no historically developed behaviors, beliefs and teachings centered on abandonment. We simply do not know what to do, or say or believe when an adult child turns on a parent. The resulting isolation is felt by parents, not only from their children, but also from friends who are unable to cope with the fact of abandonment as well.

3. Abandonment of parents by adult children is culturally prohibited and contrary to most religious doctrine. The Judeo/Christian Bible, the Koran, Buddhism and so on all has prohibitions against abandoning or disrespecting parents. Every culture has a mandate of respecting and caring for parents, the elderly and ancestors. See: "And your Lord has decreed that you worship none but Him. And that you be dutiful to your parents. If one of them or both of them attain old age in your life, say not to them a word of disrespect, nor shout at them but address them in terms of honour." (Quran

17:23) "And lower unto them the wing of submission and humility through mercy, and say: 'My Lord! Bestow on them Your Mercy as they did bring me up when I was small.'" *Sutta-Nipata*: Though being well-to-do, not to support father and mother who are old and past their youth -- this is a cause of one's downfall. (I:6, Narada Thera, tr.) ...a wise man...should support his mother and father as his duty....(II:14, John D. Ireland, tr.)   Often culturally the mandate is accompanied by a warning of the consequences of failure to care for parents. For example, the Judeo/Christian 10 Commandments contain a demand that "Honor Your Father and Mother so that you may live long in the land that the Lord God has given you." Contained within that commandment is a not so subtle hint that if you don't honor your parents you may not live long in the land. And in fact current data would suggest that adult children who have abandoned their parents do not do well in their adult lives.

4. The nature of the act is torturous and mean and generally covers an extended period of time. The mind of the adult child processes abandonment and often practices the abandonment by sequential acts over a period of time that begin with negative verbal remarks, often sarcastic, with the end game being complete disconnection to the parent in every way. It is a social and psychological process of eliminating their relationship with the parent - living a life as if the parent is deceased. This doesn't happen overnight even if at times it seems that way. Often it begins in the teenage years or perhaps it begins to be visible in even earlier years particularly in case of a nasty divorce between the parents. The "walking on eggshells" is often another first sign of the beginning of the estrangement process. The longevity of the abuse causes permanent brain damage making the turning away difficult at best. Once the brain has learned a behavior it is difficult to turn the thought processes toward enough positive thought to begin healing.

... is there an island for castaway moms,
Far far away from dolls and little toy drums.
Is there a land where Cast-a-ways go,
To live free of pain and judgment and woes?
Is there a sea of velvet and pearls,
Where Castaway moms can also be girls ?
Is there a place of wonder and awe
Where memories freeze and never unthaw ?
Is there a planet under the sun
Where Castaway moms can live with fun

Is there a yonder over the blue?
Where sadness can't enter for me and for you?
Here I sit a Porcelain doll, tossed over there
Against the wrong wall.
Please pick me up and help me to play
I just cannot do this, not one more day!

By Cambridge Keenan

5. Parents who have lost their children through abandonment cannot progress through the normal grieving processes. Most people live in a cause and effect world. While there is always some ambiguity about 2 + 2 equals 4, mostly it works out that way. When children abandon their parents with such cruel intentionality it destroys the cause and effect world in which that parent has lived and found identity. It works like this: I

raised my child as best that I could, I tried to make the right decisions, provide what my circumstances allowed me to provide, made my share of mistakes and none of this adds up to the venal ostracism that I am now experiencing from this offspring. It is an equation that does not work and nothing the parent can do can make it work. If we live in a tit for tat world then what shortcoming or action on the part of the parent would justify cruelty and abandonment? Somewhere in the brainy thought processes of the adult child there is a twisting, a click off of reality and socialization that makes their behavior not only acceptable but preferable.

6. Research shows that ostracized people will seek to gain re-entry by becoming submissive and in that submission lose their identity. Most parents are reduced to begging, crying, showing their pain to the child, bargaining, giving more, tolerance, walking on egg shells but nothing helps to alleviate the behavior or the pain. It seems that these grieving behaviors only serve to aggravate the adult child and drive them further into indifference. As a result, parents become stuck losing their self-confidence and drastically shifting the power of the parent/child relationship to the adult child. The parent becomes less in his/her own eyes while simultaneously embolden the adult child who seems to feed off the pain. Adding the destruction of the cause and effect formula to the elimination of identity and nurture of family and we have a human being outside any normal processes of grieving and recovery. These processes do not engage in this scenario. There are no casseroles brought to the house by the neighbors, notes of condolences, flowers, and a ritual of burial. Worst of all may be that friends and neighbors begin to pull away because they don't want to hear your pain or the conversation threatens their own parent/child relationships or they begin to think there was something the parent did to deserve this treatment. So the parent begins to live their grief in isolation daring not to mention it once again to close

friends. Sometimes parents just wear their friends and supporters out because the grief process never ends and can go on for many, many years. Indeed to the end of their lives.

7. Abandonment is symbolically the ancient scapegoat ritual in which the designated goat is driven out of the community and destined to wander the world alone and diseased while remaining alive and aware of its isolation. Definition: A scapegoat is person or group that is forced to take the blame for happenings that are not their fault. Commonly, in many different cultures, when a unit, family or otherwise, becomes anxious someone is targeted to become the scapegoat and is designated to be exorcised. It happens at work, at play and in families. Once a member of a family has become the designated scapegoat they are banished, avoided and unapproachable.

Dysfunctional people and families that are steeped in shame, and cannot look at their issues often engage the scapegoat ritual as a means of healing. They have poor insight into their own behaviors and problems, and will do anything to appear normal or exceptional, despite the fact that in reality, they are terribly crippled by their fears, addictions, mental disorders, abuse, neglect and insecurities. The scapegoat is an advertisement for suffering. The goat must live and wander about so that so all may see the unhealthy part of their community or family as outside of themselves. Sometimes when a family unit becomes very anxious, both because of alienation or mental illness or some kind of trauma, the breaking point occurs and someone has to leave or be expunged. This is how the scapegoat ritual occurs in families. An example of that is a family that has lost a child due to an accident of some kind. It frequently occurs that the parents' divorce as the family unit cannot contain or resolve the anxiety and grief that occurs from the loss.

The scapegoat ritual plays a part in the parental alienation syndrome along with the false images and language used to alienate. In fact alienation occurs when the deliberate conduct on the part of the alienating parent works and then the non-alienating or target parent is shunned and sent away. The child is then relieved to get back to a sense of normalcy and lack of anxiety which was brought on the stress of the broken and toxic relationship. So the parent who is alienated is sent away and like the wandering goat must not be approached again. The mere sighting of the alienated parent causes an instant anxiety reaction and a rushing away from that "sacrifice". Indeed the only normalcy for that alienated child, adult or otherwise, is to be out of sight and out of mind of the "sacrificial goat" or in today's terms the "targeted parent."

Once again, I thought that I was strong enough to look up my estranged child on Facebook. Look at the pictures and walk away. I don't know why I don't just block my estranged child and walk away. After a 4 year estrangement, You would think that I would know better and that it would test my heart to see if I am truly over her. I am trying but it is just too much to see pictures. How do you stay away from FaceBook or how do you deal with what you see?

8. Abandonment becomes a physical and psychological wounding which often trains the brain of the parent to re-live the traumas, succumb to diseases and dysfunctional states of being physically and psychologically. Ostracism and loneliness produce a flurry of activity in the brain associated with alertness and cognitive function. These areas of the brain are associated with issues such as PTSD, ruminating and obsessive thoughts, Alzheimer's, depression and suicidal ideation. The toxic stress produced by abandonment and abusive treatment is associated with heart attacks and inflammation in the body

both of which dumps all sorts of deadly hormones into the system to sludge things up in there. These conditions deepen as a person ages. In fact, the emotional fallout is so poignant that the brain registers toxic stress as physical pain. Imagine treating a person so harshly that it causes them physical pain. Mortality is estimated to be reduced by 11.8% by mere loneliness itself. More and more research today shows a definitive connection between both mental and physical disease brought on or exaggerated by the toxic chemicals produced by the stress of grief and alienation. The brain areas most affected support a variety of functions, including emotion, behavior, motivation, long-term memory and olfaction. This area of the brain, which becomes damaged, appears to be primarily responsible for emotional life and it has a great deal to do with the formation of memories

There is evidence that learning and repetition expands, anatomically, some areas of the brain. However there is a growing body of evidence relating to PTSD specifically that new and deleterious paths are laid down and/or enhanced by certain bad experiences.

So to be clear, the abuse of abandonment, ostracism and cruelty on the part of adult children toward their parents is a major brain injury that produces real and definitive brain changes and damage including all aspects of emotional and physical health. The major brain trauma exaggerates aging and produces measurable disease and diminishes pleasure and happiness in the parent.

Further, the intensity of these consequences are often felt more harshly by parents who have experienced other traumas in their lifetimes such as being abused as a child, war, addiction, accidents and earlier losses such as the death of a child. And always the consequences of trauma are individualized; some feel it more than others. The extent to which stressful events have lasting adverse effects is determined in part by the individual's biological response (mediated by both genetic predispositions and the availability of supportive relationships that help moderate the stress response), and in part by the duration, intensity, timing, and context of the stressful experience.

9. The abandoned parent becomes debilitated by the major anger issues that approach rage and the oppressiveness of that rage prevents or delays the onset of positive thought. Anger is a destabilizing emotion and eventually needs to be mediated. It is reptilian for a parent to protect its offspring. Pictures of wild animals roaring over the lost of their child or a threat to their child's safety are firmly embedded into the mind of all of us. It is a terrifying image of seeing a female holding the body of her dead child and roaring in pain. When a child turns its back on a parent there is anger directed toward whoever has hastened that departure as well as at the child. The parent however fears releasing or expressing the anger as they acquaint showing anger with the destruction of the hope of reconciliation. Another one of the hurdles to healing is that the abandoned parent hardly finds a safe place to talk about it, express that anger and release it. Our best friends and acquaintances often don't want to hear it anymore because of their own worry that it could happen to them. Further the rage stage can last years. It is a rare parent who can move through any healing process quickly. The norm is years. And that is a long time for friends, pastors or therapists to hang in there with you. Those experiences of rage coupled with abandonment, lostness often cause the abandoned parent to experience rumination about the events and words experienced during their relationship with their child. Going over every word, every event, every nuisance, they become obsessed with these thoughts, lose sleep and functionality. Caught up in a web of warding off the barrage of false accusations that destroy their self-image experienced in a world of strangeness and rumination they often sink into depression and suicidal thoughts and further isolation from society. This grief becomes their own private hell.9.

10. The consequences to the parent of abandonment are biologically, spiritually and physically inconsistent with life. Traumatic brain damage, obsessive-compulsive thoughts, suicidal ideation, physical infirmities are natural companions of the alienated parent. These parents are victims of hate crimes. And where is God in all of this? Indeed where is God in all of this. Standing in a pulpit preaching forgiveness with no audience. So to say, as we did in the beginning that abandonment of parents carries a death sentence is true again and again. A parent who has this experience often dies a horrible death spiritually, socially and sometimes physically. There is nothing worse than dying alone with no one to bury you. It means that you have no home to go to where they have to take you in. It means that you have no immortality or sense of it – no generational place.

11. The level of hope that it takes to believe in the possibility of reconciliation dies very slowly. The stories of reconciliation of abandoning children are very, very few and usually relegated to short term estrangements. The same is true for the fantasy held by many abandoned parents regarding a future relationship with grandchildren. Once a core belief is established and firmly embedded justifying the abandoning of parents, the chances of reconciliation are very slim. However, the abandoned parents remain committed to a core belief that loving their children unconditionally will somehow sustain them. Unfortunately, this core belief of unconditional love condemns the parent to a long term experience of toxic stress. The reality is that most parents could not even bear the thought of their children returning as the reopening of the wounds that have only slightly scabbed over causes an overwhelming anxiety reaction. The ultimate end then is that the rift cannot be healed because the one is so damaged they have lost their capacity to heal and the adult/children are so riddled with anxiety that they are imprisoned in the confines of their own history. Both states of being and both states of

raw woundedness illustrate the extent of the trauma. A friend who works in post-traumatic stress disorder warned us, quite gravely, of the risks when people visit scenes of past troubles; of hyper-arousal – sweats, nausea, and high heart-rate. Or the opposite, hypo-arousal: a state of lethargy, a feeling of unreality.

"Some of you were genuinely happy for me that my ED is in town & that we planned to meet. I saw her 3 times. It's not estrangement, but it's not like it was with the closeness. It seems she doesn't "get it" yet, will not apologize for the terrible behavior on her part that led to the estrangement. Also, she will not be alone with me & always has the boyfriend by her side. When she was a teen, she'd do that with a friend or boyfriend after she'd done something her dad or I would take issue with.

She now puts me in the category of people who want her time while she is in town visiting. Although she will be in town til Sunday, I feel like making no more contact. I got a sharply rebuking text this morning saying how busy she is & how her phone is blowing up with people wanting to see her while here. I'm not "people". I'm the mother who loved my only child beyond measure, who always put her as my #1 priority. Now it seems as if I'm somewhere below the top 20 in her priorities. I just need to let her go, wait for her to mature (she's an immature 23) & adjust my priorities. As most of you know, just contact is not necessarily satisfying."

Leaving Your Abusive Children: The Devil's Dilemma

For all victims of abuse the first advice given is to leave the relationship. Removing the victim from the situation of abuse either though shelters, divorce, police intervention or changing of residences has always been the first avenue of rescue. But what if those abusers are your teen age or adult children? The abused parent is stuck in a situation of horror that relentlessly and systematically pounds down the psychic minute by minute until virtually nothing is left of the parent. This phenomenon is more common that the general public would know and that the government agencies have the time or money to cope with. It is an evil of humiliation, mockery, repeated and unrelenting trauma producing a state of being that is only descriptive of victims of torture.

The overriding dilemma is how can the parents bear to walk away from their own children and under what circumstances? How can the parents who have been responsible for the protection, nurture and care of their children now expose them to public criticism by openly making public their abuse?

Attendant to these prime issues is the toxic environment of shame and guilt and blame with the resulting indecision that finds the souls of parents wandering about lost in a morass of endless self-doubt. The entire science of victimology is brought to bear in multiple doses when the victim is being tortured by their own children. Scapegoating and outright lies are the weapons of these abusers seeking to justify their acts of abuse whether physical or emotional. There is no justification for abuse. No one deserves it.

The initial and perhaps long term mode that most victimized parents grasp onto is deluding themselves into believing that these children will "grow up" and realize that they have behaved badly toward me and they will change and then everything will be ok. It is the *song of the soul of estranged and abandoned parents* always to have in the back of their minds that whatever unacceptable behavior their children are engaged in it is probably age appropriate and they will grow out of it. Someday something will "click" and they will come home begging our forgiveness, which we will readily grant. Aren't we all deluded by the "teenager" philosophies and pseudo psychologies of today that explain patiently to us that "teenagers" are just a little mad and if we "pick our battles" and believe in their initial "goodness" that there will be reconciliation in paradise when their brains become adult and embrace us once again? For a good many parents this is not true and is not a common outcome today.

Society at large and their mini-society of friends and family barrage these abused parents into a never ending cycle of abuse by not even being able to imagine that children would viciously and systematically denigrate their parents unless those parents "did something wrong" or "there is always another side to the story", which is reinforced by the abusers themselves because they inevitably, like all abusers, find a litany of rationalizations about how their parents "deserved" the ridicule, ostracism and hypercritical conversations. The generation of baby boomers grew up with lots of false thoughts but among the worse was that parents were wholly and entirely responsible for how their children "turned out". If anything went wrong it was the fault of the parents – who over indulged, under indulged, and were too strict, not strict enough demanded too much, not enough, or who just had bad behaviors themselves so their children were just little copies and so on. Thank you world of child psychology. Also listening to these modern thoughts were the children who in many cases saw an opportunity to inflate their egos and engage in entitlements and self-righteousness that has awed our generation.

So the first order of business then is to look at the parents and ask "What did you do wrong?" The mere asking of that question implies that abandonment and abuse of the parent is justified if they "deserved" it. But then no one deserves abuse regardless of what they did or did not do. And we are ready always to secret away our condemnation of these abandoned parents because we harbor a belief that they did abuse their children solely based in the accusation of same. Of course, the parental victims have been asking that question in their minds through the mutual filters of shame and blame every day of their painful lives. Our society rewards adult children abusers richly for "being abused" or "coming from an abusive background". We are ready to excuse any behavior no matter how malevolent if the abuser has been "abused". We mitigate or excuse murder, torture, abandonment, ostracism, physical torment of all kinds, blaming and worse emotional blackmail, if only we can find that one hook known as the 20th century abuse marker. Well, certainly we believe today that once a child is abused it goes on to become an abuser. But is that a certainty and is that always a connection bonded in concrete. Of course not. We all know that, however it is the current sound bite that causes our knee jerk reactions of blame and further ostracism and thus we lock abused parents into relentless and systematic torture. It is virtually impossible to have a conversation about adult children abusing their parents without an instant, without a pause, inquiry as to what did the parents do to cause this conduct. The relationship between parent and child is sacrosanct and our culture, or most cultures, are seemly unwilling to consider abusive conduct in any professional manner outside the realm of blame assignment. One only asks to reflect on the early days of the social focus on domestic violence and remember what the initial societal response was to the disclosure of spousal abuse: "What did she do to deserve it?" Or in the modern phraseology of today," What was your role in that?"

Of all the heart wrenching painful soul stopping experiences that life has to offer us losing a child is considered the worse one historically. It is unimaginable to most parents. It is said that you "never get over it". A child should not "die before its parents". People who have lost children to accidental death or disease or war are destined to relive it every day of their lives. They become walking testaments to a life lost. They look forward to death so they can have a reunion with their child who has passed before them. Thus the death-dealing dilemma of the abusive relationship with adult children is that the only avenue of relief is for the victim to fully embrace and elect one of the worst experiences in life that any parent can imagine – the loss of a child. For no matter how severe the abuse the parent remembers the little guy or girl who they held in their arms and loved and were willing to give their lives to protect. How is it even imaginable that parents must bring themselves to tell their living adult child to go away and never return? "When children are young they sit on your lap, when they are grown they sit on your heart" is an old wisdom that seems true at times.

Of course there is a parallel here with any abuser/victim relationship where the victim has difficulty separating themselves from the denial of victimization and their "love" of the abuser. Heart wrenching as the abusive relationship is leaving is more unthinkable. You can go out into the world convincing yourself that you can find another husband but you can't go out and find another Timmy or Sally or Joey. It is just this dilemma that places parental abuse into the most death dealing dilemmas of a lifetime. How could one live with the knowledge that your child is not dead but exists physically somewhere and, in order to save your own life, you cannot touch or see or feel them ever again. You cannot speak their name or put a picture of them in your living room. The abused parents must chose to live in estrangement and die alone in many cases. In other words does leaving the abuser really bring with it relief and a return to wholeness or is it just another self-inflicted form of abuse called ostracism. Whether voluntary or not ostracism is torture experienced as physical pain by the human brain. Grief becomes frozen and irresolvable.

It is a puny thing to say that it ruins the remainder of the life of the parents. To be abused by ones own children is the most awful and devastating experience that an adult can have. How do you walk away from parental love? How indeed? What form of madness is this? Most parents will choose to live a life of pain rather than emotionally walk away from their children. And this is the devil's dilemma by whatever name it is called — unresolved grief, unresolved loss or empty hope.

"I was abandoned by my daughter 6 years ago this June. I received a text message that said "The keys are under the mat I have moved out, don't coming looking for me I never want to see you again you have ruined my life". I worked 50 miles from home drove like a bat out of hell at over 100 miles an hour got home and found my husband standing in her empty room. He said "did you get a text?" We looked around our house, she had taken between 3 and 5 thousand dollars from our safe (money my husband had been saving for college), she took all documents that said she was our child. She left behind all of her clothes and her backpack from school - she had just graduated from high school one week before. In her backpack we found her plan for moving out - with the help of her boyfriend and his mother - they rented a U-Haul and his friends moved stuff from our home and his mother drove her to the bank where she cleared out all of her accounts. The next day we changed the locks on our house and cancelled all of our support for her to start college that summer at the University of Arizona in Tucson (where we live). She had a prepared speech that she emailed to me - she did even say Mom or Dad anywhere in it - it was **** or my husband's first name. She stopped communicating with me about 1 year after - but each time I asked why I got the prepared speech or some slung together four letter words that I didn't appreciate. She is my only child - I have nothing else in my life. I have been secretly mad at my husband for 6 years because he did nothing to stick up for us as parents - all he said was "She 18, I was expecting this." I wasn't. I have said was "She 18, I was expecting this." I wasn't. I have gained 150 pounds and I am mentally tortured each day by the episode. I gave away all holiday decorations we don't celebrate anything anymore (to my husband's relief because he hates holidays of any kind). I have worn the ears off of all that I could tell this too and I am embarrassed to go to church and have not been in 6 years. I don't like children or teenagers anymore and I cannot stand celebrations at work - retirements, birthdays, holidays and such and have asked my co-workers to not invite or expect me to participate. My health is poor and I have become a recluse not going anywhere or doing anything anymore. I don't think I spend more than 5 minutes outside my home when I am not working. I try to make myself believe that I can overcome this - but I fail. And last night was particularly bad for me because I found out she had graduated from the University of Arizona with a bachelors in Family Studies and Human Development. All of my life I wanted to be a mother and celebrate those milestones in a child's life and she has chosen to take that away from me."

IT SEEMS LIKE IT IS A PROCESS

When adult children become estranged from parents, it seems, for some, like it happened suddenly. One moment there is the historical loving adult child and the next moment he/she is replaced by a snarly, grunting human being completely unknown and unknowable by his/her parents. It is difficult to believe that could happen overnight and it probably doesn't. It may be a process hidden from sight especially when it results from third party interference.

Many parents trace this snarly attitude (hypercritical, sarcastic, and moody) from the teenage rebellious years and say that it just never got better. It would seem that this might be true for those adult children who just didn't make the turn into adult hood. Addiction, failure to attach, failed adult children, mental illness all are causes that might lead to a visible pattern of alienation and eventual abandonment.

However there are signs that there is a process and it may look like this:

1. The beginning of attachment to an outside force whether that is alcohol and drugs, a bad peer group or a third party intervener.

2. Minor criticisms that show up as snide remarks and when confronted a refusal to discuss them.

3. A feeling of walking on egg shells, which is itself a form of abuse. Again when confronted with questions like "Is there something bothering you?" "Is everything alright?" "You seem preoccupied, what is going on with you?" there is a refusal to discuss the behavior, a dismissal of the questions and sometimes an angrier response.

4. There may be alongside of these feelings the beginning of the non committal phone calls that go like this: "Hello Honey,

how are you?" "Fine" "What is going on?" "Nothing" "Did you get the package I send to you?" "Yes" "Did you enjoy the cookies?" "Yes" and so on.

5. After that the excuses begin for not attending a holiday tradition or family event. Letters go unanswered. Grandparents and uncles become incorporated into the non-committal conversations and begin to wonder what is going on with the adult child.

6. Phone calls go unanswered. Letters unanswered. When phone calls are answered it is as if it was an accident and they are on the way out of the door, no time to talk. At this point the relationship changes to a somewhat hostile response to the parents.

7. The hostility increases, accusations against the parents for childhood neglect and or abuse begin.

8. There is a cessation of contact sometimes accompanied with a proclamation about how the parents deserve this. Generally this signals that their loyalties have found an attachment somewhere else.

9. The adult child begins to behave as if the parent is dead and gone. At this point the relationship has become one of complete abandonment. Any contact is met with extreme hostility, sarcasm and cruelty.

10. If the adult child marries or has children there may be a brief period when parents are included but it is always carefully supervised and riddled with negativity. The parents are made to feel as if they are there for show and nothing more. Parents sometimes trace the beginning of estrangement when there are third party interveners back to the initial meeting of the prospective daughter or son in law where there seemed to be an "edgy" feeling surrounding the first and subsequent meetings.

There is a case to be made for the sudden estrangement and abandonment of parents but it is almost always associated with a third party intervener such as a new son in law. Although some parents who feel that their estrangement was sudden might has just missed the clues since it is unimaginable that it could happen and parents shrug off the signals as age appropriate. In any case the estrangement process feels like a slippery slope when viewed in retrospect.

<u>HEALING BEGINS</u>

What does it take to find a life after abandonment, after prolonged trauma, after the inevitable illness that follows that trauma? It seems to many of us that the grief is irresolvable and it goes on day after day and most probably night after night and there is no solution except the daily coping with nagging pain and perhaps the urge to take our own lives. But there is healing to be found and what is proposed here are just a few things that have worked for others. However nothing listed here is a substitute for professional help or medication for that matter especially if you are feeling that you want to take your own life. Please seek professional help immediately if you begin to feel that way.

You might find that in the beginning the grief is so overwhelming that taking an initial step toward getting better seems impossible and in many ways it is. Begin with whatever you have to begin with in terms of energy, attention or time and turn your thinking towards wellness. It is ok that you can only manage a tiny step. It is ok that the tiny step is not more than a sigh and a glance out of the window.

With that said, here are some practices that have helped others. Not the only path perhaps but a path that just might lead you to a partially restored life and even partial happiness. This path does not require a heroic effort to "get over it" nor does it require a well formed intent or super human will power. It is ok to just drift into it giving yourself all the time it takes. Respect your injury.

It begins with expectations and our expectations must be thought out and understood and re-understood throughout the remainder of our lives. What is possible and what is not possible must be accepted in the heart, soul and mind of each of us. Those expectations are framed by understanding that the pain will always be there, that suffering is a state of being that will always beckon to those whose children have left them with a trashed life and broken heart. "The process of overcoming is endless. Overcoming is not resolution. Overcoming is a looping process where a dominant emotion has to be overcome by its opposite and it is the opposites that are bound together.(Roland Gilbert)" It is not about will power or faith or self-esteem. It is about our humanity.

Hope and its role in your recovering life

Hope is defined as the feeling that what is wanted can be had or that events will turn out for the best. Hope is akin to wanting to win. So we know that hope is a feeling, an emotion. So what we can hope for is this: that we will recover from this trauma - that we will build a new life - that we will discover our purpose and we will live a meaningful life. Hope cannot be allow to imprison us with the commitment to something that we have no control over such as a future reconciliation where we again live in paradise with our adult children. Hope is the only reason you won't give in, burn what's left of the ship and go down with it. (Barbara Kingsolver)
So don't give up on yourself or your life.

The normal process of ostracism and it's awful consequences

From an important study by Kipling Williams and Steve Nida we learn the dynamics of ostracism and how it threatens 4 basic human needs: a sense of belonging, self esteem, a sense of control and a sense of meaningful existence. When a member of any group senses ostracism it is all 4 of these needs that are threatened and we as human beings have a natural, instinctive way to correct the ostracism. We begin a series of behaviors seeking to rescue our place in the group, ways to regain lost control. Sometimes those behaviors do not facilitate inclusion such as striking back or lashing out but does restore a sense of control. Aggressive behaviors also force the group to recognize the existence of the ostracized person which is probably why the ostracized person does them. However, long term ostracism may deplete the individual's resources that are necessary to fortify the threatened needs and can lead to a sense of alienation, helplessness and depression. Interestingly, these same behaviors are consistent with the symptoms of Post Traumatic Stress Disorder. There may be a connection between the initial aggressive behaviors and a depletion of resources. It takes a lot of energy to continue aggression and the constant and inevitable rejection of those aggressive behaviors is a mini re-wounding each time they are displayed.

Eventually after long term ostracism, the person accepts the essential message of their ostracism and that they are completely insignificant and worthless. They experience a sense of alienation and aloneness that dominates their life. These wounded people will now ruminate on everything they did wrong and evidentially accept that the alienation is completely their fault. They seem then to self ostracize perhaps in a misguided effort to prevent further rejection from the hands of others. In this resignation stage individuals may become overly compliant or violent as well as vulnerable to fringe or cult groups. The violent aspect of this research is particularly bothersome. It might be that violence is more prevalent in younger adult children than older ones. Mr. Williams and Mr. Nida did not consider in any great detail the unique plight of abandoned parents.

So for purposes of healing, our resources must be directed toward replenishing the basic needs identified by this model. We need a sense of belonging, a healthy sense of self, a sense that we have control over our lives and a meaningful life. These are categories for healing and we must look for ways to buttress and restore and replace whatever served those needs before the traumatic event of abandonment. First however, we must find a way to step away from the crushing pain that renders us inert and find a way to reach out and save ourselves. Not an easy task to accomplish.

First Educate yourself about the abandonment as a shared phenomena.

First, or perhaps first coupled with other things, read books, articles, blogs whatever source gives you left brain information about your situation and the reality of the abandoned parents. Go to seminars about parents left behind. Blogs that encourage you to share pain and experience are often helpful. There are several on Face book: Parents Abandoned by Their Adult Children; Support Group for Parents of Estranged Adult Children. Daily Strength: Parents of Estranged Children Everywhere. On the Internet: www.abandonedparents.net. Look at the end of the book for a thorough listing of Face book pages. There is a book list attached to this book.

The suggestion here is to find <u>intellectual information.</u> How does abandonment happen? What are the dynamics? Sometimes when the pain and confusion are so great finding a path through the left brain is an easier beginning than trying to deal with the overwhelming emotions attached to the loss.

Next use your imagination to take the pain down a notch and get yourself started

When the pain is so great that you think you cannot stand it begin here: The beginning of a healing quest is always the most difficult in a process. How do you get started in the process of alleviating pain and suffering which has erased not only your personality, your identity but also the purpose for your life? We begin with envisioning – a process that lets our soul speak through imagery (Sometimes times called directed prayer). Begin to use your human ability to create, project and live in imagination. Close your eyes, see yourself in a dark, but not scary, place. Slowly fill in the darkness with a picture in whatever ways your heart is leading. [1] Notice the details of this dark place. Is it a room? Forest? Closet? Is there a window? A moon? Are you sitting on a chair? The ground?, and then imagine a golden path beginning to emerge, faintly at first but then getting brighter with each breathe. It is leading you somewhere. You think (still with closed eyes), maybe, it is leading you out of the darkness. Just look at it for a while, you may not want to do more than observe but then slowly think about taking a step to follow it. Gently, tentatively at first, take the step. Watch yourself slowly walk down that golden path, slowly, reassuring yourself at every moment, taking all the time you need. Where does it lead? Notice what is around you – sounds, smells, objects. You can repeat this process everyday creating your own private place. Let this place teach you. Keep a journal.

Another healing Image is to see yourself sitting in a windowless room, devoid of furniture or other things. It is very grey in that room, is it cool or too warm, what smells are present, do you hear anything? Do you recognize the room? Then, when you think the time is right imagine that a window appears on the far wall. Watch the window for a while until you feel like you want to walk over to the window and open it just a bit; feel the fresh air that gently flows in from the outside, what do you see? Imagine the warmth of the sun that enters the room. Very gently, quietly stay with the imagery until the window opens by itself completely and you begin to feel the sunshine, the smell of the fresh breeze and slowly but slowly fill the room with your favorite things, your things and no one else. Make this your private place, your healing place. Go there every day. Keep a journal. Let your soul speak to you.

You may want to keep this imagery with you as you learn from the books and resources you are reading. Ask yourself what am I sensing from partnering the learning and the imaging. Learning that you are not alone and beginning to understand what has happened to you and your children will be slow and that is ok. You may want to keep these two processes to yourself, let them teach you, become familiar with them. There is plenty of time for sharing after you get some solid foundation. Sometimes sharing too early dissipates the energy of these beginnings. Do not expect miracles but always be open to the possibility. Those of you who are spiritual may want to pray during this process. Try the 23rd Psalm or this Morning Prayer:

Dear Lord, I thank You for the Grace of being alive this morning; I thank You for the sleep that has refreshed me; I thank You for the chance to make a new beginning."

Next you will need to change how your brain is thinking about your abandonment

Here are four thoughts that will help change how your brain is processing the information about your abandonment. Practice, practice, practice these thoughts and at the same time you repeat them, try to believe them. Your brain is like any other muscle in your body it can be trained to perform better and more productively. One of the habits of our brain is that it converts repeated information to belief statements and that it like to form habits in how it processes information. However it is possible to change those habits and belief statements into healthier and more helpful ways of functioning. Once you practice these thoughts and you begin to see the wisdom and the reality in them your brain will start to incorporate them into the story you tell yourself about your abandonment.

**** this is all new to you. It's only been the first year of missing your daughter. It doesn't get easier and the more you reach out the more obnoxious they get. My daughter called me every day of her life if not spent time together. She even called on her honeymoon. We did everything together her whole life. I was a young mother, only 18 and I pretty much grew up with my daughter as my companion in everything, always including her friends as well. Now I've suffered every birthday, hers, mine and the two granddaughters alone thinking what the heck went wrong. Christmas is a joke. I sold all my decorations at a garage sale. They were all brand new just for the girls with a train and all. Thanksgiving is just another day as is Easter. Try therapy. I did and what I got out of it was just an hour a week to vent. He

honestly didn't have a clue how to help me. We couldn't point at one action and say that's the problem so let's fix it.

I dream about my daughter as a young child and all the good times we had together. Sometimes it feels healing, others I wake yearning for what was and is gone. I dream of the grands, the years of parenting them while my daughter and son in law worked and played. I had just finished chemo when she got pregnant and never had a chance to really recover before I was babysitting first one and then two and it kicked my butt. They would leave here and I would be drenched in sweat and exhausted from chasing them around and entertaining them.

I know a lot of what happened came from her newest group of friends. She never kept friends but dumped a group to move on and hang with a different crowd time and time again. The last group was rich snobs and she was suddenly a snob just like them. I felt unwelcome among this group and snubbed at events at her house the last couple of months. I did find that she took the girls out of private school and not public school. Grandma wasn't buying them clothes and stuff anymore. Other then that I have heard nothing through the grapevine. She has everyone too scared to tell me anything. I can only imagine what she said about us. Hang in there Anna. It takes a long time to find even minutes of peace each day and some days none at all. Over four years and I can sometimes go a week without crying. Hang in there

1. Recognize that the children you grieve are not those that currently own their names and faces.

We grieve the historical child. The one who sat on our lap and listen to the stories we read - the one that we played peek-a-boo with. This is not who they are today.

2. Realize that your story goes on without them and your story is valid and valuable.

You had a life's purpose, an identity, dreams, a sense of humor before you had children and while those children may have caused you to completely change your identity, you can have your story back and you should.

3. Realize that you life you create is not inferior to the one you thought you would have had with them.

So society tells us that family, grandchildren are predicates of happiness and we wholly incorporate that identity into our being. That is not the only path to happiness and to a meaningful life. You can create a new life that is just as fulfilling as the one you believe has been taken away from you.

4. Recognize that your children have the right to deal with the issues presented by their family of origin just as you did.

We all inherit the issues our parents were unable to deal with. We all inherit issues from our parents. We did and our children did. We dealt with our family issues the way we chose and probably the way we thought best. Our children also have this right whether they do it the way we would choose or not is their business.

5. Realize that your children occupied but a brief time in your life and you in theirs.

There is more to the experience of being and your purpose for being than that brief window of time of active parenting.

Deal with your emotions – all of them

Give full range to your emotions – all of them especially anger. Rage bitterness and righteousness. Don't be shamed into giving up your right to be outraged at what has happened to you at the hands of those you loved the most and trusted with the essence of your life. Read Shakespeare. Stand in an open field and while shouting fully, read the Book of Jonah to the sky. Write poetry about your grief and don't worry whether it is good or bad poetry and then publish your poetry on line with your name on it. Don't dwell on forgiveness or concepts of being positive because without a full expression of your feelings these are shame producing thoughts. You aren't there yet. <u>And never, never let anyone engage you in conversations about how you should consider your "role" in your abandonment.</u> Run those people off with a stick. There is time for positivity and an analysis later but now experience the essence of the life threatening injury you have received. Rage it in voice and in words. Get it out of the shadows. Allow yourself to experience the betrayal, the cruelty and the horror. Eventually you will want to let go of the rage but at the proper time and place. You will need to make it sit in the back of the room so you can go on with your life. If, however, you deny the experience the anger will not leave you and it will harm you with physical disease producing inflammation and a brain addicted to ruminating thoughts.

Very important to get your life under control

One of the issues created by frozen grief is obsessive ruminating thought patterns. It is in part a brain habit which you must change over time – slowly, always think slowly. So the brain exercises above help but we also know that stress can agitate and trigger the brain to bring on these obsessive and toxic thought habits.

So it is critical to form an intention to live a stress free life, avoid toxic inquisitive people, and don't get too tired, too hungry or too thirsty. This kind of grief pain is sneaky and it pounces on you when you are most vulnerable. It seems like in times of stress toxic people are drawn to us which just makes everything worse. These toxic people may be new or old friends. Regardless of which avoid them with or without explanation. **You will not get well in a stressful environment.**

One of the mysteries of life is that worry and grief come at you full forces at night time especially after you go to bed. So if you wake up at night and can't sleep, get out of bed immediately. Do not lie there and ruminate as that will only help your brain practice its obsessive grief habit. Leave the bedroom and go do something physical - mop the floor or clean a closet. Sleepiness will return and you can go back to bed. If you have to, in the beginning, take a mild sleeping pill to get you started on this way of dealing with the night terrors. Understand that you are fighting for your life here and do what it takes to defeat lying in bed at night and suffering.

Each time the pain and anguish returns, do yoga breathing strenuously, blow out the pain and ruminating thoughts, blow it out, not meekly but profoundly with each exhale. Use these exhales as a shield from the negative energy that comes to claim you. When you exhale imagine that you are exhaling the pain. Tell the pain to go away, demand that it leave you, and shout it out if necessary. This is a good place to use your rage. Tell those thoughts to get the hell out of your head. Fight for your life.

Defend your peace! Do not give it up quietly. Remember the poem of Dylan Thomas "Do not go gentle into that good night. Rage, rage against the dying of the light." Demand that those reoccurring thoughts and feelings leave you and not return. Continue this practice until it works and the time you make for this personal torment is reduced to seconds.

Meditate, meditate, meditate and yoga

You will not be able to control the anxiety and pain of this grief without meditation. This is a bold statement clearly but a true one. Drugs will not do it in the long run and have very bad side effects. Meditation of any kind repeated as many times a day as necessary and for as little as 10 minutes will reduce to manageable levels anxiety and pain and the feeling of aloneness. You can see results quickly but don't stop. Probably you will need to use meditation for your life time. Remember here we are not dealing with a static loss. The loss of our children is a daily event with varying waves of intensity. Again defend your health practice. Turn off the phone. Tell people in your household that when you close the door you are not to be disturbed.

Yoga goes along with meditation and it doesn't matter which type of yoga you chose from going to a class or watching the practice on YouTube. Do it daily.

Make these two disciplines a life saving habit and it will do just that – save your life, refresh your brain and mediate the pain. The abandonment by your children and the consequences of that to your mental and physical health demands on going practices to mediate the daily stress and pain.

Find a spiritual practice

Find a spiritual practice and go there every week. If that is a church or synagogue or a yoga room or just a particular tree in the park where you go and sit silently, form the habit and go there. Participate in the spiritual or religious practice but not to the point where your obsessive thinking habit finds another outlet. Obsessive thoughts are like flood water – if you dam them up one place they quickly find another place to flood. In the beginning those thoughts will look for another outlet so they can stay alive and religion is one place they particularly like. Don't let that happen as it will delay your healing. Keep some respectful distance from the faith practice. Be patient with the organization you chose. As always go slowly. Faith is for most of us a necessary part of healing.

If you are fortunate enough to live near an African American church with a good choir and a great preacher in that tradition, you might find it very uplifting to attend. The African American citizens know what your suffering is like and they have developed one of the best healing processes for coping, for hope and for justice yet to be seen in the spiritual community. Thanks be to them. If you do not attend such a church, you can find this tradition on YouTube where you can listen to gospel music in and to some sermons. However, there is no substitute for being there. Maybe they will let you sing in their choir.

IN THE DEPTHS OF PAIN GET OUT AND LOOK UP

Sometimes when it hurts so badly it is unbearable, move yourself. Get out of the house and look up at the trees, walk on the beach, in the woods, along a road. Find beauty in a snow storm, get wet in the rain, let nature embrace you and comfort you. And walk and walk and walk until you are too tired to feel the pain. The point here is not to allow this intense pain to take up residence in your house where you are establishing triggers which cause your brain to relive these events. It is possible to dissipate this energy by going outside and looking up. Remove your physical self from the point of the attack of grief. The quicker you can sense the oncoming pain and react by leaving the house and moving outside the less frequent and less intense these events will become.

Avoid emotional charged activities

Carefully engage emotionally charged situations with an eye toward avoiding them. If you are on a board that argues and quarrels all the time with a massive dose of political intrigue – Resign. Limit activities to those that are soothing and predictable. Every highly charged emotional environment will delay healing and cultivate your brain habit of ruminating obsessively.

Cultivate a "give a damn" attitude. Do you have a dog in that fight? Are you the person to take on that particular conversation or not? Avoid controversial leadership? Will you remember this event a year from now? Are you in conversation with a friend who constantly tells her story of intrigue and negativity? If you answer yes to any of these questions, get out of it.

Cherish yourself and only carefully engage negativity when absolutely necessary and do it only on your own terms. Tell your friend who repeats her negative intrigue daily to you, that you are going through some changes in your life and need to have a different subject matter when you are together. If you are on a board, an officer in an organization, a leader at work, reframe, moderate, resign, pass off and avoid should be your key words.

Think of it this way, if you have pneumonia would you go to a kindergarten class full of children who have runny noses. No, of course not. It is mandatory that you recognize that you are deeply wounded and that restoration to wholeness is critical and that it will take time. Nothing is more important than that, not even a career.

Try to stop making the "crazy" model

One of the common accusations made by adult children is that the parent is "mentally ill", "unstable", or just "crazy". Unfortunately the research shows that when people become ostracized the first stage of reaction is to try anything to get back in the group or unit. We beg, bargain and cry. We plead our pain and ask anxiety producing questions, make accusations and get angry. This behavior is very normal and this is what our brain wants us to do. However, it re-enforces the very behavior the adult children claim to be the reason for the abandonment. So this normal intuitive behavior needs to be stopped immediately. Further research with alienated children in divorce situations demonstrates that the parents who behave the opposite of the other parent's accusations are the ones who reconcile with their children most frequently. So if the accusation is that my mother is mentally ill because she is depressed all the time. Do not act depressed, even if you are, in the adult child's presence or in any one else's presence that might report it. If the accusation is the mother flies off the handle in anger, don't fly off the handle. You get the point here. Demonstrate purposefully the behavior opposite to that of which you are accused. This is very difficult.

Posters, web sites, Face book, notes, cards,

Do not read posters that say your life is completely a result of choices you make or listen to people who say things like that to you. These are subtle messages that push you toward self hate and shame. The voice goes like this: "Oh my god, why can't I choose to be positive/healthy/forgiving? There must be something wrong with me." The internet is full of posters of uplifting and inspiring quotes, pictures, sayings tied to cute puppies and kittens, scenes of wild life and sunsets. Learn to discern which ones are good for you and which ones are not. They are all mixed in together and they are a constant subliminal source of information that trains your brain muscle. The abandonment by your adult children is not your fault; there is nothing you can do to change it. There are some things you can do to moderate the injury.

You may want to make a computer file of uplifting messages, posters and quotes so that you can return to it when needed. YouTube allows you to compile a list of your favorite songs – also an uplifting thing to do. Both of these files can be a resource for you when the grief moments hit and you need to immediately direct yourself toward healing.

Al-anon has a small booklet called "One Day at a Time" with daily short readings. While it is geared to addiction I found it very helpful to start the day with a message of courage and meaning.

The internet also has several "positive" daily messages you can sign up to receive. Tut, is one. The Daily Good from The Unbounded Spirit is another. It is remarkable how opening your internet each day and finding uplifting and wholesome messages addressed to you can start the day off on a good note.

Avoid triggers and if can't avoid them embrace them

An alienated parent once wrote that she spent a day researching where she could go to avoid any semblance of Christmas celebrations. She was sadden when she learned there really wasn't such a place in the world except in the lonely confines of her own home, with the blinds drawn, the radio and television off. Even that didn't work for long as the minute she left the house the images were everywhere. Birthdays, holidays, weddings, funerals, baby showers, and pictures of the children and the grandchildren are all sources of deep pain and grief and they are very difficult to avoid. It is the holidays and birthdays that bring you to your knees every single time.

But you can avoid some of them such as weddings and funerals and other family parties. Do not make yourself a target at these events. Just give yourself permission not to attend. Let your adult children explain why Mom and Dad aren't at his wedding. It is so difficult to say no to these family events especially those that you have anticipated all of your life such as a graduation or wedding. Weigh carefully the price you will pay for walking into those situations.

Birthdays, theirs and ours, are especially difficult when we are forced to remember our children by that ever reoccurring event on the calendar. Remember that their *birth*day was also an event in your life as well. So why not have a *birthing* day celebration. There is a Facebook page titled The Birthing Celebration that will give you some ideas. Bake a cake, celebrate bringing new life into the world, play popular music from that year, have a party. Reach out to someone who you were friends with back then. A child's birthday is something to celebrate that is yours and no one should take that wonderful event away from you. You brought life into the world and there is no greater achievement.

So do what you can to embrace these days, settle for less than the full blown joy that you had before you were abandoned. Yes and welcome what joy is available to you instead of resigning yourself to the pain and aloneness.

Some of the literature will tell you to form new rituals on holidays. Find a new family to celebrate Thanksgiving. This is very difficult. Friends will invite you over to dine with them and their children and grandchildren. Sometimes that works and sometimes it is salt on the wound. In any event it is exhausting and has the interesting effect of erasing the memories of the good holidays with the tediousness of trying to replace them. Keep experimenting until you find what works for you. You may volunteer to hand out meals in a homeless shelter, invite friends over or go to a movie and avoid the whole thing. There is a way to find some joy in these days and it takes experimenting to find it.

Then there is the awful problem of pictures of our children and grandchildren. Should we take then down, tear them up, hide them in a closet, or keep them on the shelf to look at every day? Here is what one parent did after removing from the house family pictures for years, hiding them in drawers. They found a religious statue of Mary hugging a child. It was painted silver and devoid of obvious religious symbolism. It was placed on a table alongside small framed pictures of their children in their youth when they were most remembered them fondly. Next to that the parents placed a beautiful wooden picture frame without a picture. That frame contained their hope that maybe someday their family will come back and they could take a family picture and put it in that frame. They have been able to live with that display. It is in a quiet corner of their home so they don't have to answer a lot of questions from strangers who might notice it. It is the only place where hope for reconciliation is allowed to live in their lives. Acknowledging you have children. It is the second or third or fourth question always asked of us, isn't it. Do you have children? Where do they live? What do they do? Do you have grandchildren? And so, there you are in the midst of lying, shading the story or confessing to strangers about your estrangements. It is awkward and painful. One man of about 75 who hasn't seen his only child for years, after many attempts to reconcile with him, has given up. When he is asked about whether he has children. He says no and he means it. It is possible to say that it is an awkward subject for you and you prefer not to engage it.

Sudden meltdowns

It happens whether from triggers such as seeing your adult child at a mall with the two grandchildren you have never met, or finding something in the house belonging to a child that you had forgotten. Sometimes you are just going along minding your own business and the full impact of your grief hits you like it was a heart attack. There is a feeling of sudden panic, wanting to scream and run away and shortness of breath. When these abandonment attacks happen try this:

1. Take an aspirin or whatever mild pain killer you take. Remember that abandonment is registered as physical pain in the brain.

2. Sit down, do yoga breathing and try to tell your brain to calm down.

3. Go to your folder of poster messages and go through each and every one of them.

4. Listen to some old gospels tunes about grief and power and overcoming.

Soon these panic or sudden attacks will pass. It is awful and frightening but it happens and it likely will continue to happen hopefully less and less often. Again find your practice and do it whenever these symptoms occur. You might want to speak to a doctor if they happen often as it could be signs of Post Traumatic Stress Syndrome. (PTSD)

Friends, family, therapists and clergy

Be very careful about who and where you share your painful story. If you hear a person to whom you are sharing say anything of these phrases, (and I don't care who), "There are always 2 sides to the story" or some version of "What was your part in this?" or "What did you do to them?" **Do not share anything else with that person.** They are not a person of comfort and will hurt you, usually inadvertently. They are people who are untrained in this form of estranged relationships.

Try not to share casually with friends as you are putting a "filter" in your relationship with them and then you both feel compelled to talk about it. It can begin to define your relationship with them. You may lose friends and probably will as not many others are able to cope with these stories or the intensity of your grief. And remember what Snoop Dog says, "If you ain't loosing friends, you ain't growing up."You will be surprised about which of your friends stick with you and which ones do not. Learn to discern who you can trust and who you can't.

Also be very careful about whose messages you hear. Everyone will want to help in the beginning and unless they have been there, the advice isn't usually very good even if their intention is. Likewise clergy and therapist aren't always the best people to share with unless they have been educated about adult children who abandon their parents. Otherwise they are trying to apply traditional talk therapy techniques to a situation where talk therapy doesn't help very much especially in the beginning.

All of that said, sometimes counseling helps just to be able to vent if nothing else. Medicine does not help for more than a few weeks and long term medicine, like antidepressants, generally puts off the grief, numbs your senses and puts you in a Zombie like state. Tempting though a Zombie like state is, that state of being is not a life. Make sure that the therapist you chose is educated in this problem. Sometimes a spiritual director is a better choice over a regular therapist and if you check around you can find one.

There are also grief coaches who are quite helpful. They are generally religious people who are trained to walk along side you while you negotiate the path of your loss. Make sure you find a trained person who is certified and if the match doesn't work speak up quickly.

Linguistics can change the world

If you change the words you use in your daily life you will change your brain and your life. Concentrate on these words everyday: kindness, graciousness, gentleness and mercy. You may find other words that are helpful to incorporate into your daily conversation. It is difficult at first; you may have to write then on a sticky note to remind yourself. But practice them. And then the most amazing things happen, your world begins to change to accommodate these new ideas. It works. This is very similar to concentrating on the 5 thoughts that change your brain.

Build another family

Build another family. This concept is repugnant at first but you will find that a family of sorts begins to come into your life particularly as your healing matures. Maybe this family is not a traditional one, maybe this new family is a young family who moved in down the block and has no one near to them, maybe it is an immigrant family who begins to attend church, maybe a youth group you involve yourself in, a group of friends who band together to live out their years. But a "family" will appear and will gather round you and supply you with all you need. This new family will not be a substitute as nothing can substitute for your own children but it will give you something you need which is a sense of belonging.

You may find that you begin to cherish every human being you meet however casually in a more intimate way. Connect with their struggles and let them see that connection and carrying through your smile, your graciousness and your kindness. You may begin to find the tools to connect more deeply with those already in your life as well.

Write out a personal belief statement

This is probably the most important way to find a soothing and healing pathway out of the grief and also the most difficult one. If you spend a lot of time doing it, the reward at the end is greater strength and a bolstered command of your facilities. No one will ever hurt you so deeply again, no one will ever own you because you know who you are and what guides you. So write out a statement about what your core beliefs are and then review them often. It is a struggle but well worth it in the end.

And example is this: **I believe that every living human being on the globe is entitled to decent housing, nourishing food and medical care.** So you can immediately see from this statement of belief that your behavior, your thoughts, your political and religious activities are dictated by this belief. Your brain will reject arguments that are inconsistent with this belief statement and seek out arguments consistent with it.

Another example might be this: **I believe every human being has the inherent right to determine who they associate with in their lives.** So you can see that your activities would dictate how you interact with the world and your activities would be consistent with your belief statement. The explanations you will place upon seeing another human being make an association choice will be according to your belief statement and not according to your emotional feelings.

The benefits of acting from a place of core beliefs helps bypass emotional and ego oriented explanations that we put on others who we observe acting in ways that are confusing to us. Humans like to react to what we observe by quickly processing what we see through our history of similar observations whether these pasts insights are correct or healthy. So acting from a belief position helps to avoid some of the hurts that we might otherwise experience.

Well, this is very difficult to do but critically important to avoid being whipsawed during vulnerable times in life. Getting help to write your belief statement is fair and rewarding.

Avoid the terminal question

Asking yourself "what did I do wrong?" invites obsessive thinking and is particularly the question that the brain likes to latch onto and ruminate. The brain then gets to spend its time culling over every second of every minute that you spent with your child, searching in vain for the very moment in which you did something to cause the abandonment. Clearly once that second is captured then the bad conduct of your adult child is your entire fault. Help is always available to urge you to ask this question of yourself particularly from your adult child's long litany of mistakes that you made. The question of what did I do wrong will push you down the well of hell from which there is no escape and no healing for yourself or your adult child. Don't go there.

In the entire world there has never been one child raised perfectly. All parents make mistakes and that is ok because it is human. Most parents do the best that they can with what they know then and what they have to do with. Maya Angelou says "When you know better you do better." The fault of abandonment is with the adult child.

The difference between a happy life and a meaningful life

"A happy life and a meaningful life have some differences," says Roy Baumeister This is an inquiry you might want to make of yourself as you journey through the pain and grief of abandonment. One of the important steps we must make is to find our purpose in life apart from our adult children – to re-acquaint ourselves with the "you" from the beginning, the wholeness of our personhood. Baumeister and his colleagues found that a happy life was associated with receiving from others while meaningfulness was associated with giving to others. How can your life develop into a meaningful one? Where can you give to others? What are your gifts? In the past have you define "happiness" according to what was put upon you in your childhood? What value can you find from this experience that will help others and yourself in the process? Can you re-connect with old high school/college friends? What books did you read before children that touched you? Listen to some music of a past era. What memories are associated with those songs? The point here is that our goal and a significant outcome of this tragic loss is to establish meaningfulness in our life - To find our purpose again and to find a reason to grow and contribute each day - To love again perhaps.

Expectations great and small

The abandonment by our children is the deepest wounding a person can experience in this lifetime as we have already discussed. It is probably unrealistic to expect that it can be completely healed even in a perfect world. Our souls remember. So for most of us a complete freedom from grief will not likely happen. We will have set backs, take the proverbial two steps forward and one backward. We will lapse into the depths of the grief again every time we have a new loss in our lives. We seem, as human beings, to have a review of loss function built into us and with each new loss we review the old ones and so that goes. What is realistic to expect is that the time we spent in complete despair will be shortened each time we are thrown back into it. We can expect that time will soften the pain a bit. However realistic we are and however skilled we are at healing, we remain wounded parents and we will end our days as wounded parents and that is just how humans process pain. One of the cautions is that we tend to negate the impact of the injury to our minds and bodies and to our enjoyment of life. Rather it is probably very important to treat ourselves as recovering from a grave illness because that is the level of self care required to move past despair and find our way to a meaningful life.

SPECULATION AND FINAL WORDS

It is easy to wonder what happened in our generation to bring about these unhealthy relationships with our children. Perhaps, it isn't new at all. Perhaps it is just more visible. Just because previous generations took the elderly into their homes doesn't mean they had meaningful relationships with them. A roof over their head and food on the table doesn't mean life sustaining interaction.

Another theory floating around these days is that it is fallout from the greatest generation. Those men and women, who took their trauma to the grave with them, never spoke of the horrors they experienced. Except to place their expectations onto their children to become the builders of the new America with a wealthy middle class, success replacing character and coupled with that inheritance the inability to express ourselves emotionally. So we never learned to reflect anything other than everything is fine. Hence we produced children who do not view us as human beings with needs and feelings.

Perhaps all of that gave rise to a narcissistic generation whose entire focus is on their happiness to the exclusion of anything we held valuable. Much has been written about the X Generation and their detachment from the values of the past.

Perhaps the unhealthy relationships between parents and children reflects the political views now being perpetrated by the media that the older generation is stealing resources from the younger generation who has been stuck with paying the bill for our medical care and social security. This view is further enhanced by viewing the senior parents as essentially useless.

Perhaps, this generation of young adults is more oriented toward electronic communication and has little use for direct conversation, connecting on seemingly useless conversations preferring sound bites over content and preferring peer relations over more intimate ones. Intimate relationships are more difficult and demanding, often frustrating, often involve clashes in time commitments and inconvenience.

Perhaps this generation of young adults does not feel vulnerable in any way that would lead to the need for connection to a larger group. Scattered tribalism is an apt description of what the current adult culture. The new for a tribe and all of its securities no longer exists so the current generation is re-creating what it means to belong. Clearly peer group approval and connection has replaced extended family.

This new generation of young parents sees their children as complete extensions of themselves and not as a part of any questionable family history. Another version of narcissism and scattered tribalism and a separation from the connection to land and place may also play a role.

Perhaps our culture has glorified family connections and relationships and we are now looking at what always has been. Could it be that families have always fallen short of connection and engaged in some form of estrangement? Perhaps we are just now seeing the breakdown of the romanticism of it.

Clearly there are many questions unanswered. Still we seem to believe in the family unit made up of generations of people who practice tolerance, engage in the rearing of children, know what to do when the lightning strikes the cherry tree and say things like "Well, that is just how Uncle Bill is..." and "This is where your great, great grandfather Richard stepped off the boat on the Muscatatuk River and built his house."

APPENDIX

A MESSAGE TO ADULT CHILDREN Who Have Abandoned their Parents

If you are an adult child who has abandoned your parent and you are reading this book you might have a flood of conflicting feelings ranging from outrage to shame. If you are so overwhelmed with these feelings that you cannot or will not consider that you could be wrong in abandoning them, then you should move on to a book or website that makes you feel better. If your feelings are so steeped in righteous indignation that self-reflection is not possible then you may want to consider some guidance and counseling. This book is not written for you and its perspective is not directed to you. If you are a bit conflicted about your judgment regarding your parents here are some hints that may be helpful:

Who is informing you?

With that said the first and most important issue to consider is who informs you regarding your relationship with your parents. The major reason that adult children abandon their parents is the interference in that relationship by third parties. These third parties may be a parent divorced from the other, a spouse, or a religious organization. These third parties may have sent you negative messages from your childhood or it may have begun in your adult life. Nonetheless these messages are consistently negative and contain "spin" of the facts and events surrounding your relationship with your parents. It is done for sinister reasons of control and domination. It is intentional and homicidal. It is important to discern in life how we are informed and by whom because it is only then that we can truly seek our own truth. People who thrive on estrangement are more abundant than you know and they will, in a most genteel way, seek to dominate you by taking you away from those who have always been your friend. It is a kind of control and narcissism in people who perpetuate these social crimes.

A word of caution comes from Richard A. Gardner, MD who wrote a book titled "The Parental Alienation Syndrome". Dr. Garner said "Only terminate your relationship with your parents in the most extreme of circumstances and only then after careful counseling and guidance from a professional." Your entire identity is tied up in who they are, their historical systems and beliefs trouncing around your family history.

Do you seek true freedom in life?

It is sometimes said that you are only truly free to be who you are once you have resolved the issues that your parents were not able to resolve. It is in a real sense the repayment for the gift of your life.

While it is important for you to process your relationship with your parents, hopefully with the help of a competent therapist specifically trained in alienation, it is just as important to immediately stop any abusive conduct or demeaning and humiliating language you habitually direct toward them. Stop hyper-criticalness and start communication.

The consequences of your actions

If the abuse is allowed to continue then at some point, you will not be able to reconcile with your parents. Your own vicious abuse and the lies you tell yourself will become a reality that will never leave you and you literally will live a lie the rest of your life. In the end if that parent dies before you have effected reconciliation then you live with this karma and unrecoverable grief the remainder of your life, scarring the generations to come after you. Nothing about an estranged relationship is static. The estrangement grows, intensifies and becomes irreconcilable not only for the abuser but also for the one abused. It expands itself to the extended family, to your own family and children and sometimes friends. It robs you of your happy memories. What was once an irritant becomes the basis for intense hatred and intense hatred is madness. The abused parent may suffer actual brain damage and early death as a result of your conduct. Two out of three alienated parents admit to suicidal thoughts.

What happens to your own children

There is some evidence that abandonment of parents is generational and if you abandon your parents, abuse them and disrespect them so will your children do likewise to you. There is additional tragedy in denying your children their grandparents effectively cutting them off from their generational history.

Where are your parents or have you lost track of them

If you have allowed your parents to just drift away without comment, begin to communicate in writing only in order to diminish the potential for anxiety. When anxiety appears try to figure out what it is telling you and why. Gentleness will go a long way in reversing the consequences of your behavior borne by your parents.

If you're distancing yourself from your parents because of their mental illness or addictions, then seek help first with Alanon. These people are quite experienced at assisting family members with these issues. You may find that your relationship may need to be in writing or on the telephone or video internet for a time. Seek the advice of your parent's therapist or your own if the parent is untreated. Just don't run away at a time when your parent may need you the most. In these relationships a good bit of the success or failure has to do with setting healthy boundaries and you probably would need help from professionals to do that. In this situation kindness and compassion should be your companions.

In every single case of a parent suffering from illness of any sort the support of family is critical to their recovery and wellbeing. This is something trained professional therapists can assist with. Would your parents desert you if you were ill?

If your estrangement from your parents is because you are too busy or they are not good enough or their behavior is embarrassing because you have moved up a notch on the social scale, then you have an ethical problem and you need to take a look at yourself and what kind of human being you are or want to be. The same would be true if the addictions are your own or if you have been unable to make your way in the world and you are ashamed. Seek help for your own addictions and for your ethical failings.

Why should I?

If you are overcome by your thoughts of rationalization, justification and believe without a doubt that your parents "deserve what they get", then know that these are symptoms and not truths. You are being blinded by hate.

In all ways seek to resolve your relationships, seek to reverse the consequences of your actions and make yourself a better person. In a short form, live in love not hate and in all ways seek to not end up with regrets.

Here is a short form list of what is happening to your life:

1. You are practicing hate.

2. You are practicing violent abuse toward your parents and to your own family.

3. The way you treat your parents causes them physical and emotional pain.

4. The way you treat your parents causes them to develop mental diseases such as PTSD, depression, obsessive thoughts, low self esteem, aggressive and self destructive behavior, distrust of entering relationships, isolation, anxiety, panic attacks and obsessive thought of suicide.

5. The way you treat your parents causes them to develop physical illnesses such as chronic toxic stress which leads to inflammation of body organs which leads to heart attacks, arthritis, and irritable bowel syndrome.

6. The way you treat your parents produces feelings of abandonment and ostracism which is experience as physical pain on a daily basis. This is torture.

7. The way you treat your parents shortens their life expectancy by 11.4%. That takes away about 9 ½ years of life on the average.

8. The way you treat your parents condemns them to living alone without close relationships experiencing severe loneliness the remainder of their lives.

9. The way you treat your parents is a hate crime against your own children and those of 3 generations to follow you.

10. The way you treat your parents condemns your own children to depression, low self esteem, the inability to love unconditionally and potential addictive behavior.

Imagine what it is doing to you and your family or better yet go to a doctor and ask.

List of Abusive Behaviors Perpetuated by Adult or Younger Children On their Parents

1. **Threats of and/or physical violence** Threats with or without the use of weapons or objects used as weapons, including hitting, punching, kicking, pushing, slapping, biting, hair pulling, shoving, shaking, choking, pinching, and burning. This may include the inappropriate use of medicine or physical restraints, force feeding and other physical punishments of any kind.
2. **Intimidations** including a constant refusal to do as asked such as going to bed, coming home, asking friends to leave, and cleaning up after themselves, not attending school/college/work or contributing to the household or participating in family activities. The children may also use humiliation and harassment, silent treatment, babying, and isolation from family and friends.
3. **Swearing at** the parent in public or privately.
4. **Name-calling or Verbal Denigration** Publically, privately or on line.
5. **Bullying** Including by text or phone. Bullying may also include the threats of withholding relationships, especially with grandchildren, or the entire family. Bullying also includes threats of publically disclosing family secrets or embarrassments.
6. **Stealing** money or property or misuse of parent's credit cards/phones/computers, illegal or improper use of the parents funds, property or assets including forging signatures, tricking a parent into signing documents such as Wills, Deeds, Powers of Attorney or loan documents.
7. **Deliberate damaging of property** especially objects held in esteem by the parent or objects necessary for the parents well being.
8. **Threats or actual violence to pets or other children**

9. **Emotional blackmail** such as the threat not to allow grandparents to see their grandchildren, of leaving and never coming back and revealing family secrets that would embarrass the parents or threatening to lie about the parents conduct toward them.
10. **Drugs and alcohol abuse in the home**
11. **Belittling Parents** in the presence of friends/other family members or in public.
12. **Benign neglect** Withholding or failure to provide the basic necessities of life (especially for the dependant elderly) or to provide these necessities in adequate quantity and in a timely manner.
13. **Abandonment/Desertion** The termination of the parental relationship characterized by the withholding of love and affection, care, communication and concern. The failure to stay in touch, attend family events or remember birthdays and other holidays. Wishing and acting as if the parent was no longer living and doing so with intent.
14. **Estrangement** The walking away from a parental relationship, a removal of themselves from the family, failure to return phone calls, answer emails/letters, remember birthdays or holidays. The withholding of presence for family events. Short and clipped answers to questions and the failure to engage meaningfully in conversation by giving the impression that the conversation is unwanted, untimely or grudging.
15. **Forced sexual contact** with any parent incapable of giving consent such as unwanted touching, assault, battery, rape, sodomy, or coerced nudity.
16. **False accusations** such as falsely accusing parents of neglect or abuse. False reporting to police or other authorities regarding abuse or the mental state of a parent. The constant excusing of the desertion of parents by claiming they were abusive thus implying they are getting what they deserve.
17. **Walking on Egg Shells** is a form of bulling in which there is a deliberate creation of an environment where the parents are made to feel anxious and uneasy about the mere possibility of the slightest error in speech or action that will

result in a sudden and complete disassociation with their children or grandchildren.
18. **The Silent Treatment** is the failure to communicate with parents while in their presence, often called ignoring them, failure to respond appropriately to questions or comments, coupled an intent to inflict anxiety and psychological harm.

Bibliography

Most Important Books:

1. Healing from Family Rifts *Ten Steps to Finding Peace after Being Cut Off from a Family Member*, Mark Sichel, and CSW.
2. The Parental Alienation Syndrome, Richard A. Gardner, M.D. *** This book is hard to find but check with Amazon for used copies.
3. The Empathy Trap: Understanding Antisocial Behaviors; Dr. Jane McGregor and Tim McGregor

Books:

1. Adult Children *The Secrets of Dysfunctional Families*, John Friel & Linda Friel

2. Adult Children of Parental Alienation Syndrome *Breaking the ties that Bind,* Amy J.L. Baker

3. Family Estrangements *How they Begin How to Mend Them How to Cope with them*, Barbara LeBey

4. Elder Abuse *Conflict in the Family* Karl A. Pillemer and Rosalie S. Wolf

5. "Bad" Mothers *The Politics of Blame in Twentieth-Century America* Molly Ladd-Taylor and Lauri Umansky

6. The Lives Our Mothers Leave Us, Patti Davis

7. The Social Animal *The Hidden Sources of Love, Character and Achievement,* David Brooks

8. The Lonely American: *Drifting Apart in the Twenty-first Century*, Jacqueline Olds, M.D.

9. Stop Walking on Eggshells, 2nd Edition Taking Your Life Back When Someone You Care About has Borderline Personality Disorder , by Paul T. Mason & Randi Kreger

10. When Parents Hurt by Dr. Joshua Coleman

11. "Adult Children of Parental Alienation Syndrome" by Amy J. L. Baker Dr. Baker indentifies behaviors often associated with adult alienated from their parents by PAS (not all alienation is PAS). These behaviors are drug/alcohol issues, lack of trust, depression, low self esteem, alienated from their own children, divorce.

Articles:

1. The Silent Suffering of Parent Abuse: When Children Abuse Parents By Lou Purplefairy

2. Mothers suffering abuse by their kids, The Sun-Herald by William Birnbauer May 22, 2005, "Seventy per cent of mothers have experienced violent behavior or threats from their adolescent children, a study reveals."

3. Older Women's Emotional Safety Plan, Calgary Women's Emergency Handbook

4. How Women Resist Abuse, Calgary Women's Emergency Handbook

5. Difficult Conversations, by Douglas Stone, Bruce Patton, and Sheila Heen

6. Crucial Conversations, by Kerry Patterson, Joseph Grenny, Ron McMillan, Al Switzler (http://www.crucialconversations.com.)

7. Parents Reconciliation with Children, sorrynotes.com/parents

8. The Power of Vulnerability, A study of wholeheartedness. Dr.Brene Brown,http://www.ted.com/talks/brene_brown_on_vulnerability.html

9. Happy images trigger sad reactions in the brains of people with severe depression, researchers have found. http://news.bbc.co.uk/go/em/fr/-/2/hi/health/3162076.stm

10. Brain scan shows rejection pain, being snubbed socially provokes exactly the same brain response as being physically hurt, say US researchers.http://news.bbc.co.uk/go/em/fr/-2/hi/health/3178242.stm

11. About.com/Post Traumatic Stress Disorder

12. http://www.psychologytoday.com/blog/evolution-the-self Leon F. Seltzer, Ph.D., who holds doctorates in English and Psychology, is a clinical psychologist and author of *Paradoxical Strategies in Psychotherapy*. Very helpful blog when you are seeking recovery

13. Ambiguous Loss: Learning to Live with Unresolved Grief by Pauline Boss, Harvard Press, 1999

14. . "Easing Tension and Stress at Family Gatherings, December 10, 2012" blog post; "Why We Suffer" by Peter Michelson. Peter is an author and experienced psychotherapist in Plymouth, Michigan

15. Psychology Today: Shunning – The Ultimate Rejection What Does It Mean When We Shun Others - or Are Shunned? **Published on February 1, 2013 by Rosemary K.M. Sword in The Time Cure**

16. Psychology Today: Shunning – The Ultimate Rejection What Does It Mean When We Shun Others - or Are Shunned? **Published on February 1, 2013 by Rosemary K.M. Sword in The Time Cure**

17. Loneliness: Human Nature and the Need for Social Connection by John Caccioppo, Journal of Science Daily, University of Montreal, August 25, 2011, Children of Depressed Mothers

18. 15 Shocking Statistics on Nursing Homes | Masters in Health Care www.mastersinhealthcare

19. Current Directions in Psychological Services: Ostracism: Consequences and Coping. Kipling D. Williams and Steve A. Nida.

Web Resources

www.abandonedparents.net This is a web site that connects to a Yahoo group where people can communicate. You must have a yahoo account but you don't need a Facebook account.

Facebook Resources and Page Titles

1. Parents Abandoned by Their Adult Children

2. Support Group for Parents of Estranged Adult Children

3. Daily Strength: Group title: Parents of Estranged Children Everywhere

4. Grands4Kids

5. Parental Alienation Dynamics

6. Grandparent Alienation Dynamics

7. Grandparent Alienation is Not Natural

8. Silent Grief: Child Loss Support

9. Victims of Narcissists

10. The Empathy Trap Book

11. Family Access: Fighting for Children's Rights

12. The Narcissist

13. Grandparent Rights Advocates National Delegation of the USA

14.
Photos in Forsaken and Estranged Parents who love their children. Sharing is Healing

END NOTES

Good name in man and woman, dear my lord,
Is the immediate jewel of their souls.
Who steals my purse steals trash; 'tis something, nothing;
'Twas mine, 'tis his, and has been slave to thousands;
But he that filches from me my good name
Robs me of that which not enriches him,
And makes me poor indeed.
Othello Act 3, scene 3, 155–161

NEW YORK — Every day for two years, he carried the toxic burden of a name that meant fraud to the world. On Saturday, the eldest son of disgraced financier Bernard Madoff hanged himself in his Manhattan apartment, another casualty in the saga that sent his father to prison and swindled thousands of their life savings. On the second anniversary of the day his father was arrested in the worst investment fraud in American history, Mark Madoff, 46, was found dead in the living room of his SoHo loft. He was hanging from a black dog leash while his 2-year-old son slept nearby. People close to him said he was despondent over press coverage of his father's case, an ongoing criminal investigation of Madoff family members in the multibillion-dollar scheme and his struggle to rebuild his life.

Center on Developing Child, Harvard University

Francis Eppes Professor of Psychology at Florida State University. The difference between a happy life and a meaningful life, 2013 *Journal of Positive Psychology*, co-authored with researchers at the University of Minnesota and Stanford.

In their never-ending search for the best way to live, Greek philosophers argued over the relative benefits of *hedonic* and *eudaimonic* happiness. Hedonic well-being sees happiness as a factor of increased pleasure and decreased pain, while eudaimonic ("human flourishing") happiness has more to do with having a larger purpose or meaning in life. A recent study from University of North Carolina at Chapel Hill psychologist Barbara

Fredrickson may reveal which form of happiness is more beneficial for health and well-being. The study, which was published in the *Proceedings of the National Academy of Sciences* last year, found that while both types of happiness can make you feel good, the latter could promote physical health and longevity as well

Anger Grade Scale: 12 infuriated; raging; rageful; boiling; explosive, 11.5 fuming; smoldering; inflamed; outraged, incensed; enraged, 10.5 seething; livid; "hot", 10 bitter; irate; inflamed; rancorous, 9.5 heated; wrathful; vengeful, 9 hostile; belligerent, 8.5 riled; galled; agitated; pissed off, 8 indignant; insulted, 7.5 disgusted; fed up; exasperated, 7 perturbed; piqued, 6.5 upset; antagonized; cross, 6 resentful, 5.5 provoked; irritated, 5 miffed; irked; chagrined; disgruntled, 4.5 vexed; "hot under the collar", 4 irritable; irascible; grumpy: grouchy, 3.5 peevish; petulant; testy, 3 offended; provoked, 2.5 frustrated; uptight, 2 annoyed; chafing, 1.5 impatient; edgy; distressed, 1 bothered; troubled, 0.5 displeased; disappointed, 0 completely calm and cool; peaceful; tranquil; fully in control—both emotionally and cognitively> Psychology Today, The Anger Thermostat—What's the "Temperature" of Your Upset? In identifying degrees of anger, "hotter" is definitely higher. Published on January 2, 2014 by Leon F. Seltzer, Ph.D. in Evolution of the Self

"Missing Matthew"

I have a memory of having a child,
When I was just a child myself,
Seems that he has been taken away,
As if he's controlled by somebody else,

I remember being a good mother,
To this child I birthed from my soul,
He has removed me from his heart,
Now my heart will never be whole,

He roams the Earth and continues,
To pretend that I don't exist,
I have to block out the sadness,
Or my soul will remain in a fist,

Negative energy drains me,
It smothers the life force inside,
I continue to breathe and rise every day,
Forcing the pain to the side,

I carried him inside for nine months,
Listening to the song of his heart beat,
When he arrived into my world,
I thought my life would be complete,

A mother can't change the direction,
That her child chooses to go,
All she can do is step back and wait,
Her heart can never let go,

Here I am where I'll always be,
Because I am your mother,
Here is where I'll wait for you,
Loving you like no other,

Here is where I'll be standing,
On that day of hope and faith,

Here is where you'll find me,
I've been here so I won't be late,

Waiting for my child to find me,
For my love has never waned,
In a second I would give you,
All my love despite my pain,

It's called unconditional love,
It comes from a mother's heart,
The day I gave birth to this child of mine,
It was given right from the start.

Written by Victoria Gauci

Author's Bio

Sharon Ann Wildey, born in North Vernon, Indiana in 1943, received a Bachelors degree in Sociology from Indiana University and a Doctor of Jurisprudence degree (JD) in 1975. She earned a Masters of Divinity degree from Chicago Theological Seminary in 1998 and was ordained in the United Church of Christ in 2002. Upon retiring from the ministry she relocated to Costa Rica. Sharon has published 5 books of poetry at www.sharonwildeypoetry.com . She also maintains a web site for abandoned parents at http://www.abandonedparents.net along with a blog which she monitors at abandonedparentsnetwork@yahoogroups.com. Sharon is the owner of a Face book page titled Parents Abandoned by their Adult Children where she provides information and coaching.

Made in the USA
San Bernardino, CA
10 November 2015